Understanding IAS 18
Revenue

By PricewaterhouseCoopers LLP's UK Accounting Technical Department
London, September 2003

Published by

145 London Road
Kingston upon Thames
Surrey
KT2 6SR
Tel: +44(0) 870 241 5719
Fax: +44(0) 870 247 1184
E-mail: info@cch.co.uk
Website: www.cch.co.uk

This book has been prepared for general guidance only and does not constitute professional advice. You should not act upon the information contained in this book without obtaining specific professional advice. Accordingly, to the extent permitted by law, PricewaterhouseCoopers LLP (and its members, employees and agents) and publisher accept no liability, and disclaim all responsibility, for the consequences of you or anyone else acting, or refraining from acting, in reliance on the information contained in this document or for any decision based on it, or for any consequential, special or similar damages even if advised of the possibility of such damages.

Appendix 1 is reproduced with the permission of the International Accounting Standards Board (IASB)

ISBN 1-84140-413-6

Typeset by Kerrypress Ltd, Luton
Printed and bound in Great Britain by Hendy Banks Colour Print.

U
R

Pai

Contents

Chapter 1

Executive summary

Scope

1.1 IAS 18, 'Revenue', sets out the accounting treatment of revenue arising from certain types of transactions and events. Revenue arises in the course of an entity's ordinary activities and is referred to by a variety of different names including sales, turnover, fees, interest, dividends, royalties and rents. IAS 18 identifies the primary issue as determining when to recognise revenue and sets out the criteria that should be used for determining whether or not revenue should be recognised. Practical guidance on applying those criteria is given, primarily in an appendix that describes a number of different situations.

1.2 The standard applies to accounting for revenue from the following:

■ Sale of goods.

■ Rendering of services.

■ Use by others of an entity's assets that gives rise to interest, royalties or dividends.

1.3 The sale of goods includes goods manufactured for sale and purchased for resale, but does not include construction contracts that are accounted for in accordance with IAS 11, 'Construction contracts'. Where services rendered are directly related to construction contracts, for example, services rendered by project managers and architects, they are also dealt with under IAS 11, rather than under IAS 18.

1.4 The standard excludes from its scope certain items that are dealt with by more specific standards, including lease agreements (IAS 17), dividends from equity-accounted investments (IAS 28) and changes in the fair value of financial assets and liabilities or their disposal (IAS 39).

Definition of revenue

1.5   Revenue is defined as the gross inflow of economic benefits during the period arising in the course of the ordinary activities of an entity, when those inflows result in increases in equity, other than increases relating to contributions from equity participants. Revenue includes only inflows of economic benefits that belong to the entity and it, therefore, excludes amounts collected on behalf of and paid or payable to others, such as value added tax or amounts collected on behalf of a principal by the entity as agent. In the latter situation, the revenue attributable to the entity is the commission that it is entitled to keep, not the gross receipts that it must pay to the principal.

Measurement

1.6   Revenue should be measured at the fair value of the consideration received or receivable. This is normally agreed between the entity and the purchaser of goods or the user of the asset. Consideration is net of trade discounts and volume rebates allowed by the entity.

1.7   Fair value is defined as the amount for which an asset could be exchanged, or a liability settled, between knowledgeable, willing parties in an arm's length transaction.

1.8   Where consideration is deferred and the arrangement is thus effectively a financing transaction, the consideration is discounted to present value. The discount rate to be used is whichever of the following is the more clearly determinable:

- the prevailing rate for a similar instrument of an issuer with a similar credit rating; or

- a rate of interest that discounts the nominal value of the instrument to the current cash sales price of the goods or services.

The difference between the fair value (that is, present value) and the nominal amount of the consideration is recognised as interest revenue on a time apportionment basis that takes account of the effective yield on the asset (the debt).

1.9 When goods or services are exchanged for similar goods or services, the exchange is not treated as generating revenue. Examples given are the exchange of oil or milk, where suppliers exchange inventories in different locations to fulfil demand on a timely basis. More recent examples might include swaps of capacity by telecoms companies or swaps of advertising by e-businesses (dealt with by SIC 31, 'Revenue – Barter transactions involving advertising services').

1.10 By contrast, when goods or services are exchanged for dissimilar goods or services, the transaction gives rise to revenue. The amount of revenue is measured at the fair value of goods or services received, adjusted for any cash or cash equivalents received or paid. If the fair value of goods or services received cannot be reliably measured, the revenue is measured at the fair value of goods or services given up by the entity, again adjusted for any cash or cash equivalents received or paid.

Identifying the transaction

1.11 Whilst most transactions are straightforward exchanges, some may involve a number of elements. An example given in IAS 18 is where a product is sold with an undertaking to provide after-sales service. In such situations, it is necessary to allocate the consideration received between the different elements of the transaction. In the example given, part of the consideration would be attributed to the servicing element and recognised as revenue over the period of the service obligation.

1.12 Other transactions may be even more complex. An example is a sale with a repurchase commitment. In such circumstances the standard makes clear that all aspects of the transaction or the whole of a series of transactions that together constitute, in substance, one transaction, must be considered. In the case of a sale with a repurchase commitment the standard notes that the repurchase commitment effectively negates the original sale. The UK standard FRS 5, 'Reporting the substance of transactions', deals in more detail with such transactions and may provide additional guidance that will be useful in applying the principles of IAS 18.

Sale of goods

1.13 Revenue from the sale of goods should be recognised when all of the following conditions are satisfied:

- The entity has transferred to the buyer the significant risks and rewards of ownership.

- The entity does not retain either the continuing managerial involvement normally associated with ownership or effective control over the goods.

- The amount of revenue can be reliably measured.

- It is probable that the economic benefits associated with the transaction will flow to the entity.

- The costs to be incurred in respect of the transaction can be reliably measured.

1.14 The standard notes that transfer of the significant risks and rewards of ownership normally occurs when legal title or possession passes to the buyer. This is the case with most retail sales, but in other situations the transfer of significant risks and rewards may pass at a different time. For example, in sales of property the equitable interest may pass when an unconditional and irrevocable contract for sale is put in place.

1.15 The standard lists circumstances in which transfer of significant risks and rewards has not taken place and thus revenue is not recognised. These are:

- Retention by the entity of an obligation for unsatisfactory performance that is not covered by normal warranty provisions.

- When receipt of revenue from the buyer is contingent on the buyer obtaining revenue from its sale of the goods.

- Where goods are shipped subject to installation and the installation is a significant part of the contract that has not yet been completed by the entity.

- When the buyer has the right to rescind the purchase for a reason included in the sale contract and there is uncertainty about whether or not such rescission will occur.

1.16 Where, however, the significant risks and rewards have passed and the entity retains only insignificant risks and rewards of ownership, revenue is recognised. Examples given of such circumstances are:

- Where the seller retains legal title solely to protect the collectability of the amount due (often known as Romalpa clauses in contracts).

- In retail sales where the seller offers a refund if the customer is not satisfied. Revenue is recognised in such situations provided the seller can estimate reliably future returns, for example, if there is an established history that supports the estimate and the seller recognises a liability for such returns based on the previous history and any other relevant factors.

1.17 Revenue is recognised only when it is probable that the economic benefits associated with the transaction will flow to the entity. The standard notes that in some situations such probability may not be present until the consideration is received or an uncertainty is removed. Where revenue has already been recognised because there was no uncertainty about receipt of the economic benefits at the time of recognition, such uncertainty may arise later, perhaps from the insolvency of the debtor. In that situation, any provision against the amount due from the debtor is recognised as an expense and not as a reduction of revenue.

1.18 The standard refers to the matching of revenues and expenses and requires that revenue and expenses relating to the same transaction or event should be recognised at the same time. Although the IASB's Framework is based on an assets and liabilities approach, reference to the matching concept is not inconsistent with this as generally application of the assets and liabilities approach will result in a proper matching of revenue and costs.

Rendering of services

1.19 When the outcome of a transaction that involves the rendering of services can be reliably estimated, revenue from the transaction should be recognised, by reference to the stage of completion of the transaction at the balance sheet date. Reliable estimation of the outcome of a transaction is possible when all the following conditions are met:

■ The amount of revenue can be reliably measured.

■ It is probable that the economic benefits associated with the transaction will flow to the entity.

■ The stage of completion of the transaction can be reliably measured at the balance sheet date.

■ The costs incurred and the costs to complete can be reliably measured.

1.20 Revenue recognition by reference to the stage of completion of a transaction is known as the 'percentage of completion' method. The method recognises revenue according to work done, that is, in the accounting period in which services are performed. As such it gives a truer reflection of performance than if revenue recognition is deferred until the end of the contract, which could be in a different period from that in which the majority of the services are rendered. It is the method used in IAS 11, 'Construction contracts', and IAS 18 notes that the requirements of IAS 11 are generally applicable to recognising revenue and costs for a transaction that involves the rendering of services. IAS 11 contains more detailed rules than IAS 18 relating to contract revenue and contract costs.

1.21 As for sale of goods, IAS 18 notes that revenue is only recognised when it is probable that the economic benefits associated with the transaction will flow to the entity. Once revenue has been recognised any uncertainty that arises subsequently and that requires provision to be made against amounts due to the entity, is recognised as an expense and not as a reduction of revenue.

1.22 A reliable estimate of the revenue to be received may generally be made when the entity has agreed with the other party:

■   Each party's enforceable rights regarding the services to be performed.

■   The amount of the consideration.

■   The manner and terms of settlement.

1.23 The entity should have an effective system for monitoring and reporting progress on the contract and should revise its estimates of the outcome of the contract as it progresses in the light of performance to date. Progress of the contract and the stage of completion should be assessed regularly to measure the value of services rendered. A number of different methods may be used, including:

■   Surveys of work performed.

■   The amount of the services performed to date as a percentage of total services to be performed.

■   The proportion of costs incurred compared to estimated total costs of the transaction.

1.24 The standard notes that in determining costs to date only costs incurred in providing services should be included and only costs that reflect services performed or to be performed are included in the estimate of total costs of the transaction. In this regard the UK UITF issued Abstract 34, 'Pre-contract costs', the principles of which may be useful in applying this part of IAS 18 and which is referred to in paragraph 5.38. IAS 18 also notes that where progress payments or advances are received from customers these may not reflect services performed, but rather may be payments in respect of work still to be performed.

1.25 Where services are provided by an indeterminate number of acts over a specified period of time, revenue is as a practical matter recognised evenly on a straight-line basis over that period, unless there is evidence that another method gives a better reflection of work performed. For example, revenue from a contract to provide maintenance services for a six-month period would normally be reflected on a straight-line basis over the six months. Where, however, in such a contract there is one or more specific part or act of the contract that is much more significant than any other, revenue is recognised in line with completion of the act.

1.26 If the outcome of a contract for providing services cannot be reliably estimated, revenue should only be recognised to the extent of costs incurred that are recoverable. This may be the situation in the early stages of a contract for providing services. Where the outcome of a contract cannot be reliably estimated and it is uncertain as to whether costs incurred to date can be recovered, such costs should be expensed as incurred. If at a later date recovery of such costs becomes probable their recovery is recognised as revenue rather than by reversing the original write off of the costs.

Interest, royalties and dividends

1.27 Revenue from the use by others of the entity's assets in exchange for interest, royalties or dividends should be recognised when:

-     it is probable that the economic benefits associated with the transaction will flow to the entity; and

■   the amount of the revenue can be reliably measured.

1.28   Interest should be recognised on a time apportionment basis that takes account of the effective yield on the asset. The effective yield is the rate of interest required to discount the future cash inflows over the life of the asset to its initial carrying amount. Interest revenue includes amortisation of any discount or premium or other difference between the initial carrying amount of a debt security and its maturity amount. The initial carrying amount of a financial asset is measured at cost under IAS 39, 'Financial instruments: Recognition and measurement', that is, at the fair value of the consideration given, including transaction costs.

1.29   When an interest bearing security is purchased, any accrued interest is allocated when received between pre-acquisition and post-acquisition periods. Only the latter is recognised as revenue with the former amount – the pre-acquisition element – being treated as a reduction in the cost of the investment.

1.30   Similarly, dividends received from pre-acquisition net income of an equity investment should be deducted from the cost of the investment. Where, however, it is difficult to make an allocation of dividends between that part which relates to pre-acquisition and that which relates to post-acquisition income of the investee, the whole dividend should be treated as revenue, unless it, or a part of it, clearly represents a recovery of part of the investment (such as, for example, a return of capital in the form of a special dividend).

1.31   Royalty revenue normally arises in accordance with the terms of a royalty agreement (for example, 5 per cent of sales made by the other party) and should be recognised on that basis, unless the agreement's substance is such that another systematic and rational basis is more appropriate.

1.32   The standard makes the same point as for sales of goods and rendering of services that revenue is only recognised where it is probable that the future economic benefits of the transaction will flow to the entity. When uncertainty arises after recognising revenue and a provision is necessary against amounts due to the entity, this is recognised as an expense and not as a reduction of revenue.

Disclosure

1.33   The standard requires disclosure of:

■   The accounting policy for revenue recognition, including the methods adopted for determining the stage of completion of transactions that involve rendering services.

■   The amounts of each significant category of revenue recognised in the period, including:

    ■   Sale of goods.

    ■   Rendering of services.

    ■   Interest.

    ■   Royalties.

    ■   Dividends.

■   The amount of revenue recognised from exchanges of goods and services in each of the significant categories of revenue.

1.34   Any contingent liabilities, such as warranties, claims, penalties or possible losses, or contingent assets should also be disclosed in accordance with IAS 37, 'Provisions, contingent liabilities and contingent assets'.

Detailed guidance

1.35   The standard contains an appendix that gives detailed guidance on specific types of transactions that give rise to revenue. These include bill and hold sales, goods shipped subject to conditions, orders for which payment is received in advance, property sales, servicing fees included in the price of a product, financial service fees and franchise fees.

Chapter 2

Introduction

2.1 The issue of revenue recognition is fundamental to reporting performance. Evidence of this has been dramatically shown by a series of high profile accounting restatements in the US and, to a lesser extent, in the UK, which have severely damaged investor confidence. The areas where restatements of revenues have been made include:

- Barter sales, for example, in advertising.

- 'Round trip' trades.

- Transactions with off balance sheet partnerships and other special purpose entities.

- Network capacity swaps.

- Recognition of sales to distributors before on-sale by the distributors.

- Improper accounting for lease income by shifting finance income into amounts recognised on inception of lease.

- Persuading wholesalers to accept inventories above normal levels and recording as sales.

- Recording sales when proceeds are subsequently invested in customers' shares.

- Recording sales in advance of signing customer contracts.

2.2 As can be seen from the above list (which is by no means comprehensive), the area of revenue recognition is one where the capacity and temptation for manipulation is considerable. It is, therefore, one of the most important areas on which accounting standard setters are focusing.

2.3   The current version of IAS 18, 'Revenue', which was revised in 1993, came into effect for 1995 year ends.

Chapter 3

Objective and scope

3.1   IAS 18's objective is to prescribe the accounting treatment of revenue from certain types of transactions and events. The standard distinguishes 'revenue' from 'income' (see para 4.1 below) and sets out criteria to be applied in determining when revenue should be recognised. It also provides detailed guidance on a number of specific transaction types.

3.2   The standard deals only with revenue and not with other forms of income (see para 4.6 below). It sets out criteria to be used in accounting for revenue from:

■   The sale of goods.

■   The rendering of services.

■   Use by others of assets belonging to the entity and giving rise to interest, royalties and dividends.

[IAS 18 para 1].

3.3   The standard specifically excludes from its scope revenue and other income arising that is dealt with by other international accounting standards or for which special industry generally accepted accounting practice exists, including:

■   Lease agreements (dealt with by IAS 17, 'Leases').

■   Dividends from equity-accounted investments (dealt with by IAS 28, 'Accounting for investments in associates').

■   Insurance contracts of insurance entities.

- Changes in the fair value of financial assets and liabilities or their disposal (dealt with by IAS 39, 'Financial instruments: Recognition and measurement').

- Changes in the fair value of other current assets.

- Initial recognition and changes in the fair value of biological assets related to agricultural activity (dealt with by IAS 41, 'Agriculture').

- Initial recognition of agricultural produce (also dealt with by IAS 41).

- The extraction of mineral ores.

[IAS 18 para 6].

3.4   Although not specifically stated in the standard it seems that it would also exclude changes in the fair value of investment property which are dealt with by IAS 40, 'Investment property'. IAS 40, however, refers to IAS 18 in respect of determining the date of disposal of investment property.

3.5   The sale of goods includes goods manufactured for sale by the entity and goods purchased for resale. Services rendered include those provided within a single accounting period and those provided over more than one accounting period. Where services relate to a construction contract, for example, services of architects and project managers, they are accounted for under IAS 11, 'Construction contracts'. [IAS 18 paras 3, 4].

3.6   Use by others of an entity's assets in the context of IAS 18 generally relates to financial assets or intangibles, as IAS 17 deals with the most common form of tangible asset use, which is leasing. For financial assets, such as loans in the form of cash or cash equivalents, charges for the asset's use are usually in the form of interest. For intangibles such as patents, trademarks, copyrights and computer software the charges may be in the form of royalties or licence receipts. Equity investments give rise to revenue in the form of dividends (but note that the standard excludes equity-accounted investments such as associates from its scope). [IAS 18 para 5].

Chapter 4

Definition of revenue

4.1　The IASB's Framework for the preparation and presentation of financial statements defines 'income' and distinguishes it from 'revenue', which is defined in IAS 18. Income is defined in the Framework as:

"...increases in economic benefits during the accounting period in the form of inflows or enhancements of assets or decreases of liabilities that result in increases in equity, other than those relating to contributions from equity participants." [Framework para 70]

Revenue on the other hand is defined in IAS 18 as:

"...the gross inflow of economic benefits during the period arising in the course of the ordinary activities of an enterprise when those inflows result in increases in equity, other than increases relating to contributions from equity participants." [IAS 18 para 7].

4.2　Both revenue and income exclude contributions from equity participants, which could include subscriptions for share capital and capital contributions.

4.3　Revenue includes only economic benefits arising in the ordinary course of an entity's activities whereas income includes such resources that arise from all activities whether ordinary or extraordinary.

4.4　The Framework explains that income encompasses both revenue and gains. Revenue arises, as stated above, in the ordinary course of business and is referred to by various names including sales (turnover in the UK), fees, interest, dividends, royalties and rent. Gains are described in the Framework as other items that meet the definition of income and may or may not arise in the course of the entity's ordinary activities. [Framework paras 74, 75].

Definition of revenue

4.5 The reference in the Framework to gains being 'other items' suggests that they are not revenue, but the Framework notes that such gains may occur, like revenue, in the course of the entity's ordinary activities. The Framework gives examples of gains. They include those arising on the disposal of non-current assets, for example, tangible fixed assets or long-term investments. They also include revaluation surpluses arising on revaluation of marketable securities or fixed assets. [Framework para 76].

4.6 It is clear that revenue excludes revaluation gains as well as contributions from equity participants and income from extraordinary activities. Gains from revaluations are not revenue, because the definition of revenue does not include 'enhancements of assets' and refers to inflows of economic benefits alone as giving rise to revenue. Gains on disposal of tangible fixed assets within ordinary activities are also excluded from revenue. The Framework points out *"When gains are recognised in the income statement, they are usually displayed separately because knowledge of them is useful for the purpose of making economic decisions. Gains are often reported net of related expenses"*. [Framework para 76]. The fact that gains may be reported net of related expenses further distinguishes them from revenue. In addition, there are specific requirements, for example, in IAS 8, 'Net profit or loss for the period, fundamental errors and changes in accounting policies', that ensure that material gains on disposal of fixed assets and other items of an exceptional nature or amount, are disclosed separately from the basic types of revenue described in paragraph 4.4 above.

4.7 Another indication that gains from the disposal of fixed assets are not included in revenue is that the standard refers to the sale of goods as including goods produced by the entity for sale or purchased for resale. Therefore, property constructed for sale and held as inventory would be included in the scope, but property held as a fixed asset would not. In addition, the disclosure requirements of IAS 18 list different significant categories of revenue that must be disclosed, but the list does not include gains from the sale of fixed assets.

4.8   IAS 18 explains that revenue includes only the economic benefits that are received and receivable by the entity on its own account. It excludes amounts collected by the entity, such as value added tax, that the entity has to account for to a third party. The standard also refers to agency arrangements and states that revenue for an agent excludes amounts that the agent collects on behalf of its principal. The agent's revenue consists of the commission that it earns for carrying out the agency function. This would certainly apply in the case of a disclosed agent, but agency arrangements can be complicated, particularly where they involve undisclosed agents and this issue is discussed further in paragraph 10.1 onwards.

4.9   Where a company sells certain items either FOB (free on board) or CIF (cost, insurance, freight), it may wish to reduce the CIF items to FOB by deducting these expenses from revenue. If there is no profit element in the insurance and freight being charged to the customer, then it could be argued that these charges are merely reimbursement of expenses and not revenue and, therefore, should be used to reduce the carriage costs included in the profit and loss account. However, where there is a profit element in the CIF charges, it may be argued that the amount for revenue should include the full CIF selling price, as the recharge of the CIF elements is effectively being treated as a revenue-earning part of the transaction.

Chapter 5

Revenue recognition

General rules

5.1   IAS 18 distinguishes between revenue from the sale of goods, revenue from the rendering of services and revenue from the use by others of the entity's assets. The principles for recognising revenue for each category are similar and are set out in the following paragraphs.

5.2   For the *sale of goods*, revenue should be recognised when all the following conditions have been satisfied:

■   The entity has transferred to the buyer the significant risks and rewards of ownership of the goods (see para 5.13).

■   The entity does not retain either continuing managerial involvement to the degree usually associated with ownership or effective control over the goods sold (see para 5.18).

■   The amount of revenue can be measured reliably (see para 5.48).

■   It is probable that the economic benefits associated with the transaction will flow to the entity (see para 5.45).

■   The costs incurred or to be incurred in respect of the sale can be measured reliably (see para 5.34).

[IAS 18 para 14].

5.3   For a transaction involving the *rendering of services*, when the outcome of the transaction can be estimated reliably, revenue should be recognised by reference to the transaction's stage of completion at the balance sheet date. The transaction's outcome can be estimated reliably when all the following conditions are satisfied:

■ The amount of revenue can be measured reliably (see para 5.48).

■ It is probable that the economic benefits associated with the transaction will flow to the entity (see para 5.45).

■ The transaction's stage of completion at the balance sheet date can be measured reliably (see para 5.20).

■ The costs incurred and the costs to complete the transaction can be measured reliably (see para 5.34).

[IAS 18 para 20].

5.4 Revenue arising from the *use by others of the entity's assets* yielding interest, royalties and dividends should be recognised when:

■ It is probable that the economic benefits associated with the transaction will flow to the entity (see para 5.45).

■ The amount of the revenue can be measured reliably (see para 5.48).

[IAS 18 para 29].

5.5 The three situations above have the following conditions in common:

■ Reliable measurement of consideration.

■ Probability that the economic benefits from the transaction will flow to the entity.

5.6 In relation to the sale of goods and rendering of services the following two conditions, which are not really relevant to the third situation, are also the same:

■ The costs incurred or to be incurred in the transaction can be measured reliably.

■ The stage of completion of the transaction at the balance sheet date can be measured reliably and in the case of the sale of goods this is the stage at which the significant risks and rewards of ownership have passed to the buyer and the seller does not retain control over the goods.

Comparison with US GAAP

5.7 By way of comparison under US GAAP, the four principles set out in SEC Staff Accounting Bulletin No.101, 'Revenue recognition in financial statements', (SAB 101) are:

■ Persuasive evidence of an arrangement exists.

■ Delivery has occurred or services have been rendered.

■ The seller's price to the buyer is fixed or determinable.

■ Collectability is reasonably assured.

5.8 The conditions in IAS 18 and SAB 101 are expressed somewhat differently, but are in essence the same. For example, persuasive evidence of an arrangement is implicit in the condition under IAS 18 for the sale of goods that the entity must have transferred the significant risks and rewards of ownership. IAS 18 notes that in most situations the transfer of significant risks and rewards occurs when legal title is transferred or when possession passes to the buyer. [IAS 18 para 15]. In the case of rendering of services IAS 18 states that the requirements of IAS 11, 'Construction contracts', generally apply to recognising revenue from a transaction involving rendering of services. [IAS 18 para 21]. IAS 11 specifically applies to arrangements where a contract is in place.

5.9 The condition in SAB 101 that delivery has occurred or services have been rendered is again consistent with the IAS 18 conditions. Under

IAS 18, as noted above, the significant risks and rewards are generally transferred on delivery or on passing of legal title. In respect of services, IAS 18 requires that the stage of completion of the transaction can be reliably measured at the balance sheet date. Revenue under a transaction involving rendering services is recognised under IAS 18 by reference to the stage of completion, often known as the 'percentage of completion' basis. [IAS 18 para 21].

5.10 The condition in SAB 101 that the price is fixed or determinable is matched by the IAS 18 condition that the amount of revenue can be measured reliably.

5.11 The condition in SAB 101 that collectability must be reasonably assured is comparable with the IAS 18 condition that it must be probable that the economic benefits of the transaction will flow to the entity. IAS 18 notes that in some situations this may not happen until the consideration is received or until an uncertainty is removed. It gives an example of uncertainty as to whether a foreign government will give permission to remit proceeds of a sale in the foreign country and states that when the uncertainty is removed revenue is recognised at that point. [IAS 18 para 18].

5.12 Broadly speaking, therefore, the approach to revenue recognition in IAS 18 is consistent with SAB 101, although there may be some differences in the detailed application. This may occur particularly in relation to the detailed interpretations issued in the US on specific issues and interpretations of the principles in IAS 18 made in the absence of detailed application rules.

Transfer of significant risks and rewards

Transfer of significant risks and rewards – applies to the sale of goods

5.13 As explained in paragraph 5.8 above in relation to the transfer of the significant risks and rewards of ownership of goods, IAS 18 notes that the transfer usually occurs when legal title or possession is transferred to the buyer. It notes that there may be other instances where the risks and rewards are transferred at a different time. One such example is given in the appendix to the standard. This is where in some jurisdictions the equitable interest in a property may pass to the buyer before legal title passes and, therefore, the risks and rewards also pass at that point. In the UK this is reflected in the practice of accounting for property sales when an unconditional and irrevocable contract for sale is put in place.

5.14   The standard also lists examples of situations where the transfer of the significant risks and rewards has not taken place. These are:

■   When the entity retains an obligation for unsatisfactory performance not covered by normal warranty provisions. An example would be where an entity supplies a new type of machine and guarantees that it will achieve a certain level of output or a refund will be given and it is uncertain whether the required level of output will be achieved.

■   When the receipt of the revenue from the sale is contingent on the buyer deriving revenue from its sale of the goods. An example would be a sale to a distributor where payment is due only if the distributor sells on the goods to a third party.

■   When the goods are shipped subject to installation and such installation is a significant part of the contract and has not yet been completed by the entity (see also para 11.4). An example would be the supply of a turnkey project where the seller is responsible for installing and making sure that the equipment is working to the customer's satisfaction.

■   When the buyer has the right to rescind the purchase for a reason specified in the sales contract and the entity is uncertain as to whether or not that right will be exercised and the goods returned. An example is goods supplied on a sale or return basis (see para 5.16).

[IAS 18 para 16].

5.15 If, however, an entity retains only insignificant risks and rewards of ownership a sale has occurred and revenue is recognised. The standard notes that in some situations a seller may retain legal title solely to protect the collectability of the amount due. [IAS 18 para 17]. In fact retention of legal title is no guarantee of collectability and the retention of title in such circumstances is normally only to ensure that the seller has a claim in the – usually unlikely – event that the buyer becomes insolvent. Retention of title clauses in contracts are often known in the UK as Romalpa clauses. Where a Romalpa clause has been inserted in a contract this does not normally affect recognition by the seller of revenue as the significant risks and rewards have still been transferred to the buyer.

5.16 Where an entity supplies goods on a 'sale or return' basis the situation is more complicated. In some situations, the entity may expect that there will be few returns and that the level of returns can be reliably estimated. In other situations, the entity may expect that there will be a high level of returns. An example of the former is where a retailer sells goods, but offers to refund the purchase price if the customer is not satisfied. In such a situation, revenue is normally recognised in full and a provision is made for the expected level of returns, provided that the seller can reliably estimate the level of returns based on an established historical record and other relevant evidence. [IAS 18 para 17]. An example of the latter situation would be where the entity supplies goods in returnable containers, but requires that the buyer pay for any containers that are damaged or not returned. In that situation, the seller would not record a sale or revenue in respect of the containers. Nor would it recognise revenue in respect of containers that are damaged or not returned until it agreed liability with the buyer, due to the uncertainty of estimation and the general principle that revenue should not be recognised, unless it can be reliably measured. See also paragraph 11.3 for practical application of the IAS 18 rules.

5.17 Although technically the seller has retained the risks and rewards in each of the above situations, the significant risks and rewards of the sales, taken as a whole, have passed in the first situation, because returns are not expected to be significant. In the latter situation returns are expected to be significant and, therefore, again taken as a whole, the significant risks and rewards have not passed to the buyer. This is the distinction between the two situations and is a practical treatment where the number of sales transactions is very large.

Continuing managerial involvement

Continuing managerial involvement to the degree usually associated with ownership or retention of control – applies to the sale of goods

5.18 Whilst IAS 18 lists 'continuing managerial involvement to the degree usually associated with ownership or retention of control' as one of the criteria to be considered in determining whether revenue should be recognised, it does not give any further guidance. *Control* is relatively straightforward, since the definition of an asset in the Framework is: *". . .a resource controlled by the enterprise as a result of past events and from which future economic benefits are expected to flow to the enterprise"*. [Framework para 49]. It follows that if the entity retains control it still has the asset and the benefit that it expects to derive from the economic benefits lies in the future. Therefore, there is no revenue to recognise until control is surrendered in exchange for consideration.

5.19 Continued managerial involvement to the degree usually associated with *ownership* is less straightforward, but it is highly unlikely that an entity would retain such involvement without retaining also the economic benefits of an asset. Nor is it likely that a buyer would allow such involvement if it had given fair consideration for the asset. Therefore, commercially any such continuing involvement to the degree envisaged should not normally occur if a genuine sale has taken place. If it does, it is likely that there are other features of the arrangement that would need to be considered. If, for example, an entity sold a hotel, but continued to manage it, that might raise the question as to whether revenue should be recognised. However, if there is a proper management agreement that provides a commercial fee to the entity for the management services it provides and any surplus on the operation of the hotel and benefit from appreciation in its value goes to the buyer, it may be appropriate to recognise revenue on the sale. The word *"may"* is used because it would also be necessary to examine whether the entity had given guarantees or incurred other obligations that would mean it had not disposed of the significant risks and rewards of the asset. An example of how continued control or management of an asset can affect how a transaction is accounted for is given below in the section 'The substance of transactions with the legal form of a lease' (see para 11.56).

Measuring the stage of completion

Measuring the stage of completion – applies to the rendering of services

5.20 The 'percentage of completion' basis is the method used to recognise revenue for rendering services. The requirements of IAS 11, 'Construction contracts', are generally applicable to recognising revenue and the associated expenses for transactions involving the rendering of services. [IAS 18 para 21]. In fact IAS 18 repeats almost *verbatim* the requirements of IAS 11 that relate to contract revenue.

5.21 In particular, IAS 11 and IAS 18 give similar guidance on determining a transaction's stage of completion, with the guidance in IAS 18 being slanted more towards the specific case of contracts for services. IAS 18 states that various methods may be used to determine the stage of completion reached at the year end and an entity uses the one that measures the services performed reliably. The key to this determination is that revenue should relate only to work that has been performed and should not include any element relating to work that has yet to be carried out. The methods set out in the standard are:

■   Surveys of work performed. The standard does not give further guidance, for example, on who might carry out such surveys, but normally it should be someone who has relevant experience and knowledge and who is acceptable to both parties.

■   Services performed to date as a percentage of total services to be performed. For example, an entity might have a three-year contract to provide environmental inspection and maintenance services on landfill sites and it is expected that over the three-year period ten such inspections involving similar amounts of maintenance will be required. If by the end of the first year two inspections have been completed it may, in the absence of other factors, be reasonable to assume that one fifth of the contract revenues have been earned and can be recognised.

■ The proportion that costs incurred to the year end bear to the estimated total costs of the contract. The standard stresses that only costs that reflect actual services performed to the year end are included in costs incurred and only costs that reflect services performed or to be performed are included in the estimated total costs. The standard notes that progress payments and advances received from customers often do not reflect the services performed.

[IAS 18 para 24].

5.22 Where performance of a single contract takes place over time then revenue should be recognised as performance takes place. For example, under a maintenance contract for six months, revenue should be recognised over the six months, generally on a straight-line basis, as the service is provided over that period (see also para 5.26 below). It is not acceptable to record all the revenue upfront and provide for the costs expected to be incurred in providing the services, because to do this would be to recognise revenue before the seller had performed any part of the contract.

5.23 The application of the 'percentage of completion' basis where the provision of services straddles a year end is considered in the following examples.

Example 1

A company has entered into fixed rate contracts with local authorities to inspect and report on local property values. Valuation reports were completed and sent out before the year end, but due to administrative problems, invoicing was delayed until after the year end.

Since the work has been completed as evidenced by the submission of the valuation reports and since the contracts are fixed rate, it is acceptable to recognise the revenue and profits on the work performed before the year end.

Example 2

The facts are the same as in example 1, except that the valuation reports were not completed until after the year end.

If the valuation project was sufficiently material to the activity of the year revenue would be recognised at the year end according to the percentage of completion basis. If writing the reports does not form the majority of the work involved, then an appropriate percentage of the total contract price, or of the costs to date against the total costs, should be taken to revenue with a reasonable margin recognised, provided the outcome can be assessed with reasonable certainty.

On the other hand, if writing and submitting the reports formed the majority of the work involved in the contracts then it would be appropriate to delay recognition until the reports were completed.

5.24   Determining the stage of completion may, in some situations, be a matter of whether a contract may be broken down into separate components. For example, in the shipping industry, ships may be engaged in journeys to more than one port, which are not completed at the year end. In these circumstances, revenue is often recognised by reference to the last leg of the journey completed before the year end, as long as there is no doubt that payment will be received. This would be on the basis that the contract is capable of being broken into separable components.

5.25   In relation to the last bullet point in paragraph 5.21 above, IAS 11 further emphasises that the estimation of costs incurred to the year end should include only costs that reflect performance to that point. It gives examples of costs that should not be included. (Clearly, however, such costs would be included in total costs to complete the contract.) The examples relate to physical construction contracts, but the principle is the same for service contracts. The examples are:

■ Contract costs that relate to future activity on the contract, such as costs of materials that have been delivered to a contract site or set aside for use in a contract, but not yet installed, used or applied during contract performance, unless the materials have been made specifically for the contract.

■ Payments made to subcontractors in advance of work performed on the contract.

[IAS 11 para 31].

5.26 Where a contract for services involves an indeterminate number of acts over a specified time, IAS 18 states that, for practical purposes, revenue is recognised on a straight line basis, unless there is evidence that some other method gives a better reflection of the stage of completion at each year end. For example, revenue from a contract to provide maintenance services for a six-month period would normally be reflected on a straight-line basis over the six months. In such a contract the timing and amount of maintenance services is indeterminate and the straight-line method of spreading revenue is the best practical method to use. However, where there is one or more specific acts during the contract that is more significant than the rest of the acts under the contract, recognition of revenue is postponed until the significant act has been carried out. For example, if the maintenance contract referred to above included a complete overhaul and inspection at the three and six-month stages, part of the revenue should be attributed specifically to those two significant acts. Half of that part of the revenue should then be recognised after the first overhaul is carried out and the remainder when the second overhaul is completed. [IAS 18 para 25].

Estimating reliably the outcome of a contract for services

Inability to measure reliably the outcome of a contract – applies to rendering of services

5.27   IAS 18 requires that if any of the conditions described in paragraph 5.3 for reliably estimating a transaction's stage of completion involving the rendering of services is not met, or if the stage of completion cannot be reliably estimated for some other reason, revenue should be recognised only to the extent that costs incurred and recognised are recoverable. [IAS 18 para 26]. IAS 11 contains a similar requirement in respect of construction contracts, but also deals specifically with the treatment of costs and states that in this situation, costs should be recognised as an expense in the period in which they are incurred. [IAS 11 para 32(b)].

5.28   IAS 18 explains that in the early stages of a transaction it is often the case that the outcome cannot be estimated reliably, but it may still be probable that the entity will recover the costs incurred to date. It states that, accordingly, the entity should recognise revenue only to the extent of costs incurred that are expected to be recoverable. No profit is recognised as the outcome of the transaction cannot be reliably estimated. [IAS 18 para 27].

5.29   Where the outcome of a transaction cannot be reliably estimated and costs have been incurred that are not expected to be recoverable, IAS 18 states that revenue is not recognised and such costs should be expensed immediately. [IAS 18 para 28]. IAS 11 says the same in respect of construction contracts and gives examples of circumstances where it may not be probable that costs will be recoverable and where they should, therefore, be expensed immediately. These examples are equally relevant to transactions for services and include costs on contracts:

■   That are not fully enforceable, that is their validity is seriously in question.

■   That are subject to litigation or legislation that could affect their outcome.

■   Where the customer is unable to meet its obligations.

■   Where the entity is unable to complete the contract or otherwise meet its obligations under the contract.

[IAS 11 para 34].

5.30   If costs have been written off in the circumstances described in the preceding paragraph and the uncertainties preventing reliable estimation of the outcome of the transaction are subsequently removed, the entity resumes accounting for revenue according to the normal rules in paragraph 5.3 above. It does not account for revenue in accordance with the rule in paragraph 5.27. That is, it does not recognise revenue only to the extent of the costs that have become recoverable, but rather recognises revenue according to the stage of completion of the transaction at the balance sheet date. [IAS 18 para 28]. Costs written off would, however, not be reinstated even if they are now considered recoverable, but additional revenue might be recognisable in respect of such costs.

Revenue from the use of an entity's assets by others

Bases of recognition of revenue from the use of an entity's assets by others

5.31   The different categories of revenue from the use by others of the entity's assets should be recognised on the following bases:

■   Interest should be recognised on a time apportionment basis that takes account of the effective yield on the asset. The effective yield is the rate of interest required to discount the future cash inflows expected over the asset's life to the asset's initial carrying amount. [IAS 18 para 31; IAS 32 para 61; IAS 39 para 10]. The initial carrying amount of a financial asset is determined in accordance with IAS 39, 'Financial instruments: Recognition and measurement', at cost, being the fair value of the consideration given and includes transaction costs. Interest includes amortisation of any discount, premium or other difference between the initial carrying amount and the maturity amount of the asset. For practical application of the IAS 18 rules, see paragraph 11.50 onwards.

■ Royalties should be recognised on an accruals basis in accordance with the substance of the relevant agreement. They are normally receivable in accordance with the terms of a royalty agreement and are recognised on that basis, unless the substance of the arrangement is such that another systematic and rational basis is more appropriate. For example, if an agreement provides for a five per cent royalty to be received on each sale by a third party it would be normal to recognise royalty income on the basis of five per cent of total sales made by the other party as notified to the entity. On the other hand, in a similar situation, an up-front non-refundable, payment might be made to the entity by the other party and then a royalty of one per cent of sales might be receivable thereafter. In that situation it would be appropriate to reflect the substance rather than the form of the agreement and spread the up-front receipt over the expected number of sales to be made in the future where, in substance, the receipt is an advance royalty. See also paragraph 11.40 onwards for further practical application of the IAS 18 rules.

■ Dividends should be recognised when the shareholder's right to receive payment is established. Normally this is when the dividend has been declared. See also paragraph 11.64 onwards.

[IAS 18 paras 30, 31, 33].

5.32 When an interest-bearing security is acquired, part of the price paid may represent interest accrued, but unpaid. When interest is subsequently received it should be allocated between the element that represents pre-acquisition interest and the post-acquisition element. The former element should be set against the cost of the security with only the latter element being recognised as income. [IAS 18 para 32].

5.33 Where dividends on equity investments (note that equity-accounted investments such as associates are excluded from the scope of IAS 18) are received that have been paid out of pre-acquisition income of the investee, they should be set against the cost of the investment and not treated as revenue. Sometimes it is difficult to make an allocation between amounts received out of pre-acquisition and amounts received out of post-acquisition income of the investee and in such situations all of the dividend should be taken to revenue, unless it clearly represents recovery of part of the investment's cost. [IAS 18 para 32]. An example where dividends would represent such a recovery would be where they are part of a scheme to return capital to shareholders in the form of a special dividend.

Reliable measurement of costs

Costs incurred and to be incurred can be reliably measured – applies to the sale of goods and rendering of services

5.34 In relation to the sale of goods produced by the entity, the costs incurred are generally the costs of manufacturing stocks, which are calculated in accordance with IAS 2, 'Inventories'. Where goods are purchased for resale the costs generally comprise all costs of purchase. Measurement of each of these types of cost is usually relatively straightforward.

5.35 The cost of providing services may be less straightforward, particularly as the period of a contract for services may span several accounting periods. Paragraph 5.20 onwards set out how IAS 18 requires the stage of completion of a contract for services at the year end to be ascertained. Also, as noted below in paragraph 5.49, an entity should have an effective budgeting system and should review estimates periodically. This applies equally to estimates of costs as it does to estimates of revenue.

5.36 IAS 11 gives considerable guidance on the type of costs that should be included in a contract and on the type of cost that should be excluded. Identifying the costs to be included is the first stage in measuring the costs already incurred and to be incurred. Once the costs have been identified measurement should be relatively straightforward as it will generally be the price paid or the production cost. However, with a contract for services there will often be uncertainty about the extent of possible overruns. This is why IAS 11 (and IAS 18) emphasises the need for review of estimates. In IAS 11 the equivalent requirements for the reliable measurement of costs stress the need for clear identification and, in the case of a fixed price contract, the need for comparison with prior estimates. The relevant requirements are:

- For fixed price contracts – that the contract costs attributable to the contract can be clearly identified and measured reliably so that the actual contract costs incurred can be compared with prior estimates. [IAS 11 para 23(d)].

- For cost plus contracts – that the contract costs attributable to the contract, whether or not specifically reimbursable, can be clearly identified and measured reliably. [IAS 11 para 24(b)].

5.37 In identifying the costs, particular care is needed in relation to pre-contract costs. IAS 11 states that costs that directly relate to a contract and that are incurred in securing the contract are included in contract costs if they can be identified separately, measured reliably and it is probable that the contract will be obtained. [IAS 11 para 21].

5.38 In the UK, the UITF issued Abstract 34, 'Pre-contract costs'. This Abstract contains some useful guidance on the nature of pre-contract costs, but is stricter than IAS 11 because it allows inclusion of directly related costs only from the point where it becomes virtually certain that a contract will be obtained.

5.39 Both UITF 34 and IAS 11 prohibit reinstatement of costs that have been written off in a previous period (when it was not virtually certain or probable respectively that the contract would be obtained).

Matching concept

Matching concept – applies to the sale of goods and rendering of services

5.40   The matching concept is a concept that is more attuned to a 'profit and loss account' approach than the 'assets and liabilities' approach set out in the IASB's Framework. For that reason it is somewhat surprising that the matching concept is referred to in IAS 18, however, it reflects the standard's age. The standard states that revenue and expenses that relate to the same transaction are recognised at the same time and notes that this is sometimes referred to as the matching of revenue and expenses. [IAS 18 para 19]. The reference is made in the context of sale of goods, but must apply equally to transactions for the rendering of services. The standard gives an example of warranties and other costs to be incurred after a sale, which can normally be measured reliably when the other conditions for recognising revenue are satisfied and should, therefore, be provided for at the time the sale is recognised.

5.41   The above example relates to normal warranties that are incidental to the sale. Enhanced warranties that are, or are capable of being, sold separately from the goods and are revenue-generating in their own right would be accounted for as separate sales or by using the component approach (as appropriate). The component approach is described from paragraph 7.1 below.

5.42   The matching concept is generally consistent, in terms of the effect on the profit and loss account, with the assets and liabilities approach. However, the assets and liabilities approach is based on whether or not an asset or liability exists and can be recognised. In the example given in paragraph 5.27 the standard requires revenue to be recognised to the extent of recoverable costs, which reflects the matching concept. The assets and liabilities approach might suggest, however, that revenue should be treated independently from costs and recognised only to the extent that it is due and qualifies as an asset (for example, a debtor). If it is not due, thought would need to be given to whether the costs incurred are recoverable and qualify for recognition as an asset (for example, inventory or work in progress) and if they did qualify would be recognised as such. The difference in the two approaches is that if the revenue is not recognisable under the assets and liabilities approach, the profit and loss account would record less income and less costs (assuming the costs qualified for recognition as an asset) and the balance sheet would record the costs as an asset rather than a debtor from the customer. It may be that in the future the standard will be brought more in line with the assets and liabilities approach, but for now the matching concept is clearly an element to be taken into account.

5.43 An example of how the matching concept rather than the assets and liabilities approach is applied is given in Table 1. Here there are significant upfront costs and revenue is recognised to the extent of the costs. Excess costs are written off.

Table 1 – TeliaSonera AB – Report and accounts – 31 December 2002

6 Net Sales (extract)

Other connection and installation fees received from new or existing subscribers are recognized as revenue at the time of sale to the extent of direct costs incurred. Direct costs consist primarily of technical installation work, changes in customer support systems, costs for modems, SIM cards and other equipment, distributor commissions and credit checks, and costs for supplying the customer with the printed telephone directory and a printed customer information package. To date, direct costs associated with connection fees have exceeded such revenues. Therefore, no connection revenues have been deferred.

5.44 The standard also notes that revenue should not be recognised when the expenses cannot be measured reliably. It states that in such cases any consideration received should be recognised as a liability. [IAS 18 para 19].

Probability that economic benefits will flow to the entity

Probability that the economic benefits will flow to the entity – applies to the sale of goods, rendering of services and use of the entity's assets by others

5.45 One of the conditions for revenue recognition is that it is probable that the economic benefits relating to the transaction will flow to the entity. IAS 18 notes that in some situations it may not be probable that the economic benefits will flow to the entity until the consideration is received by the entity or until an uncertainty is removed. An example of the latter given in the standard is where there is uncertainty as to whether a foreign government will grant permission for the proceeds of a sale in the foreign country to be remitted. The standard states that when the permission is granted the uncertainty is removed and the revenue may be recognised. [IAS 18 para 18]. Another example might be where the receipt of consideration depended on whether or not the buyer could obtain funding, in which case recognition of the sale would be delayed until that uncertainty was removed as illustrated in the example below.

Example

A company sold land to a Housing Association. At the company's year end the contracts had been exchanged and were unconditional and irrevocable, which accords with the company's usual policy for revenue recognition on land sales. However, completion is in two stages, with part of the consideration payable six months after the year end and part payable twelve months after the year end. The delay in payment is possibly linked to the development of a block of flats on the land and the housing association receiving the necessary funding to complete the project, although this is not specifically mentioned in the contract.

In this situation, although the receipt of funding is not a condition of the contract, there would appear to be significant doubt that the housing association would be able to pay for the land at the time of the exchange of contracts. Therefore, recognition should be delayed until the uncertainty is resolved. The accounting treatment is no different to that which would be required if the contract were in fact conditional on the housing association receiving funding; recognition should be delayed until the condition was satisfied or until completion if it were only then the situation could be resolved with sufficient certainty.

If, however, there wes no uncertainty about whether the Housing Association would receive the necessary funding, then all the risks and rewards of the land have been transferred at the year end, so credit should in principle be taken for the sale.

If at a later stage after the sale has been properly recognised, doubt arises about whether the Housing Association will be able to meet the payment schedule, provision against the debt would have to be made (see para 5.47). This should not, however, prevent the original profit being recognised in the absence of uncertainty.

5.46 Another example in respect of a transaction involving the rendering of services is given below.

Example

A car hire business only rents cars to people who have been in a car accident that is not their fault. Customers rent cars while their own cars are being repaired and they are not charged for the hire period. Invoices are sent to the insurance company of the driver who was at fault in the accident. Negotiations then ensue between the car hire business and the insurance company, which eventually result in the invoice being paid either in full or in part depending on the specific circumstances of each case.

Revenue should only be recognised when the service has been performed, the amount of revenue can be measured reliably and significant risks of collection do not exist. In this case, only the service has been performed at the time the invoice is raised. The invoice is merely the starting point for negotiations, which establish the amount of the revenue, if any. Until the insurance company agrees a price, the fee for the rental service and indeed whether this can be collected is not known. Since there is significant doubt about the probability of economic benefit flowing to the car hire company, revenue recognition should be delayed until the final fee is agreed by both parties.

5.47 Sometimes after revenue has been properly recognised in respect of a sale of goods, rendering of services or use by others of the entity's assets, uncertainty subsequently arises about the collectability of an amount already included in that revenue. The standard makes clear that if a provision is required as a result of that uncertainty (which might arise, for example, because of the insolvency of a debtor) that provision should be reflected as an expense and not as a reduction of the revenue already recognised. [IAS 18 paras 18, 22, 34].

Example

A company constructed and sold a property with a book value of £250,000 for £450,000 before the year end. Since the year end the purchaser has run into financial difficulties and cannot pay. The company has, however, received a £75,000 deposit and has a first charge over the property to secure the debt. It is difficult to assess the current value of the property, but it is possibly worth about £400,000. How should the transaction be accounted for?

Since an unconditional sale has actually taken place, it should be recorded as revenue in the financial statements. However, there will need to be a provision against the debtor. If the charge can be enforced and the property will be recovered, the debtor should be written down to original cost of £250,000, or to £325,000 (that is £250,000 plus £75,000) if the deposit received is not refundable. Account should not be taken of the current value of £400,000 as no new buyer at that figure has yet been found.

Reliable estimate of revenue

Reliable estimate of revenue – applies to the sale of goods, rendering of services and use of the entity's assets by others.

5.48 IAS 18 discusses the conditions necessary for a reliable estimate to be made of revenue in the context of the rendering of services, but the three conditions below, suitably adapted, are equally valid for the sale of goods and use by others of the entity's assets. In respect of the rendering of services, the standard states that the entity should have agreed the following with the other party:

■ Each party's enforceable rights relating to the services to be provided under the contract.

■ The consideration payable and receivable.

■ The manner and terms of settlement.

[IAS 18 para 23].

5.49 The standard notes that to make reliable estimates the entity should normally have an effective system of internal budgeting and reporting. Estimates should be reviewed and where necessary revised as the contract for services is performed. However, such revisions do not necessarily indicate that the outcome of the contract cannot be reliably measured. [IAS 18 para 23].

Chapter 6

Measurement of revenue

6.1   The general principle set out in IAS 18 is that revenue should be measured at the fair value of the consideration received or receivable. [IAS 18 para 9].

6.2   In the measurement rules laid down by the standard the concept of fair value is used extensively. The definition of fair value is similar to that used in other international standards, which has become well understood. The definition is *"the amount for which an asset could be exchanged, or a liability settled, between knowledgeable, willing parties in an arm's length transaction"*. [IAS 18 para 7].

6.3   Where the consideration is in the form of cash or cash equivalents (as defined in IAS 7, 'Cash flow statements') receivable at the time of the transaction or shortly thereafter, the fair value is generally the amount receivable. Where, however, such consideration is deferred and the arrangement is thus effectively a financing transaction, it is necessary to discount the consideration to present value in order to arrive at fair value if the effect of discounting is material. IAS 18 requires that the rate of discount should be whichever of the following is the more clearly determinable:

■   the prevailing rate for a similar instrument of an issuer with a similar credit rating; or

■   a rate of interest that discounts the nominal amount of the instrument to the current cash sales price of the goods or services.

[IAS 18 para 11].

6.4   In many situations, entities will sell the same type of goods on a cash or a credit basis. In such situations, the cash price equivalent will normally be the more readily determinable indicator of fair value. The difference between the discounted amount (that is, the fair value) and the nominal amount is treated as interest income and accounted for in accordance with the requirements of IAS 18 (and IAS 39) for such income.

6.5   When goods or services are exchanged for goods or services of a similar nature and value, the exchange is not treated as giving rise to revenue. The standard gives an example of such exchanges. This is where suppliers of commodities, such as oil, swap inventories in different locations in order to ensure continuity of supply to customers in different locations. [IAS 18 para 12].

6.6   Where goods or services are exchanged for goods or services of a dissimilar nature, the exchange is treated as giving rise to revenue. The revenue is measured at the fair value of the goods or services received, adjusted by the amount of any cash or cash equivalents received or paid. If the fair value of the goods or services received cannot be reliably measured, the revenue is measured at the fair value of the goods or services given up, again adjusted by the amount of cash or cash equivalents received. [IAS 18 para 12]. Examples of barter transactions that have been particularly common in recent years have been swaps of advertising by e-businesses and swaps of capacity by telecoms operators. The former is dealt with specifically by SIC 31, 'Revenue – Barter transactions involving advertising services'. Exchanges of goods or services are considered further in paragraph 8.1 onwards.

Chapter 7

Separate components

Transactions involving several components

7.1   In some situations a transaction may be divided into various parts or may be capable of being divided into separable components that could be contracted for separately. IAS 18 states that in such circumstances it is necessary to apply the recognition criteria to each component separately in order to reflect the transaction's substance. It gives an example of a product sold with an obligation for subsequent servicing and states that the amount attributable to the subsequent servicing should be deferred and recognised over the period during which the service is performed. [IAS 18 para 13, App A para 11]. This is illustrated in the example below.

Example – separate components

A company supplies equipment and in addition provides a maintenance service for a year. The price of the equipment and the maintenance package is £100,000. The company also provides maintenance services and equipment sales separately. The price of maintenance contracts is £10,000 per annum, and the cost of the equipment when sold separately is £95,000. Therefore, the equipment and maintenance, if purchased separately, would cost £105,000. How should the sale of the equipment and maintenance package be accounted for?

It is possible to purchase the equipment and the maintenance separately, and it would seem right to assess the contract as having two separable components, the equipment sale and the maintenance contract. It may be reasonable to assume that the 'discount' of £5,000 that the customer obtains by buying both components may be applied rateably so that the equipment should be attributed a price of £100,000 $\times$ £95,000 $\div$ £105,000 or £90,476 and the maintenance contract would be attributed a price of £100,000 × £10,000 ÷ £105,000 or £9,524 making a total of £100,000. The £90,476 would then be treated as revenue for the sale of the equipment and taken to the profit and loss account on delivery, whilst the £9,524 would be taken to income evenly over the 12 month period of the maintenance contract.

7.2 Another example might be a mobile phone company, which packages within a single contract a handset, some line rental and some pre-paid calls. If these three elements are also available separately their stand-alone prices may be a good guide as to how the contract price could be allocated between them.

7.3 At the start of the contract, the handset will have been delivered, but provision of the line and the calls will be outstanding. Thus no revenue will be recognised immediately in respect of the last two elements. Instead the revenue from line rental will be recognised on a time basis, and revenue from the calls on a usage basis.

7.4 The extent to which revenue is recognised in respect of the handset will depend on its value when separated from the line rental and prepaid calls. If it can be used with more than one network, it has a value to the customer when separated from the associated line rental, so the customer could reasonably have bought just the handset. However, if the handset can be used only with the associated line rental, it would have no stand-alone value, therefore, no revenue would be recognised in respect of the handset alone. Where a handset is sold with no associated line rental and, instead, cards with prepaid units are purchased by the user, revenue would be recognised on the sale of the handset. Revenue from the sale of prepaid units would be deferred and recognised as the units are used. Table 2 is an example of such a policy.

Table 2 – Swisscom AG – Annual report and accounts – 31 December 2002

Revenue recognition (extract)

Revenue from prepaid call cards is deferred and recognized at the time the customer makes a call.

7.5 Sometimes, when a contract has been broken down into separate components, some of those components are immaterial. In such a situation, it may be reasonable to recognise all the revenue when the contract has been substantially performed, that is ignoring whether the immaterial element has been completed or not. An exception to this would be when a contract contains a 'trigger event' before which the customer would pay nothing (see para 7.9 below).

7.6 The principles in IAS 18 would require that each separable component is measured at its fair value. However, in some situations a measurement issue may arise. If the contract value exceeds the sum of the fair value of the separable elements it may be that the additional amount is attributable to some other factor, such as the activity of managing the two elements. In that situation, the management activity will only be performed when the separable elements, and thus the full contract, are substantially complete. Therefore, it is at this point that the additional revenue attributable to the management element is recognised (see example in para 7.7 below).

7.7 The contract value, on the other hand, may be less than the fair value of the separable elements. In such a situation there may be some double-counting of elements, for example, there may be set up time that would be incurred were the components to be performed separately, but which is only needed once when the components are part of the same contract. Such double-counting should be eliminated and any single element that remains (for example, of set up time) would be apportioned among the separable components. If any remaining discount occurs, that too should be allocated among the separable components (see example 2 below). The basis of allocation could be by reference to the profit estimated for each component. (Any loss on the overall contract should, of course, be recognised at the outset.)

Example 1

A company normally carries out site clearance activities as its sole activity. However, it agrees to clear a site and then order and install two prefabricated buildings for use as temporary offices.

Separate components

It charges £50,000 for the whole contract. This can be broken down into £10,000, which is the charge it would normally make for the site clearance, and £38,000 for the two prefabricated buildings (cost of £30,000 to the company plus a normal mark-up on such buildings based on its normal profit margins). The balance of £2,000 is attributable to the management of the contract to ensure that the buildings are available at the right time and that the clearance work is designed to ensure that the buildings can be properly installed and positioned.

The revenue recognition pattern will allow the revenue from the site clearance to be recognised when the work has been performed (subject to there being no provision in the contract that no payment is due until the contract is finished, that is, no trigger event – see para 7.9). The revenue for the buildings and for management of the contract would then be recognised when the buildings are delivered and installed and the contract is, therefore, complete.

Example 2

A company sells boats for £30,000 each. Additionally, at the customer's option the company will provide mooring facilities for £2,000 per annum. The company also sells these goods and services separately. If a purchaser of a boat takes up the offer of mooring facilities there is a 5% discount on the whole package. Thus the 'package' costs £32,000 less 5% or £30,400. The normal profit margin on the boats is 20% and the normal profit margin on the mooring is 60%. How should revenue be recognised?

The discount in this case is £1,600. The normal profit element on the boat is £5,000 and the profit element on the mooring is £750. Therefore, the element of the discount attributable to the boat is £1,391 and the element of the discount attributable to the mooring is £209. The revenue recognised on the sale of the boat should, therefore, be £30,000 – £1,391 or £28,609, which would be recognised on delivery. The revenue recognised on the moorings would be £2,000 – £209 or £1,791, which would be recognised evenly over the year for which the mooring is provided.

Note: In this example the 'discount' has been allocated by reference to the normal profit margin on the separate elements. This differs from the approach in the example in paragraph 7.1, which allocates the discount in proportion to the revenue from each element. That approach could also be adopted in this case and the method used above is only to illustrate that other approaches may be adopted that are equally valid.

7.8　　Table 3 illustrates an accounting policy for transactions where there are separable components. Although this is a company reporting under UK GAAP, the policy would comply with IAS 18. The policy has been reproduced in full as it illustrates several other issues discussed in this book.

Table 3 – ARM Holdings PLC – Annual Report – 31 December 2002

1 Principal accounting policies (extract)

Turnover

Turnover (excluding VAT) comprises the value of sales of licences, royalties arising from the resulting sale of licensed products, revenues from support, maintenance and training, and consulting contracts and the sale of boards and software toolkits.

Each licence is designed to meet the specific requirements of each customer. Delivery generally occurs within a short time period after signing. Licence fees are invoiced according to an agreed set of milestone payments. Typically the first milestone is on signing of the contract, the second is on delivery of the customised technology and the third is related to acceptance of the technology by the licensee.

Revenue from the sale of licences is recognised on a percentage-to-completion basis over the period from signing of the licence to customer acceptance. Under the percentage-to-completion method, provisions for estimated losses on uncompleted contracts are recognised in the period in which the likelihood of such losses is determined. The percentage to completion is measured by monitoring progress using records of actual time incurred to date in the project compared with the total estimated project requirement, which corresponds to the costs of earned revenues.

Separate components

Revenue from per-use licences is recognised when the product is accepted by the customer.

Where agreements involve multiple elements, the entire fee from such arrangements has been allocated to each of the individual elements based on each element's fair value. Vendor-specific objective evidence of fair value is determined by reference to licence agreements with other customers where elements are sold separately.

Agreements including rights to unspecified products are accounted for using subscription accounting, revenue from the arrangement being recognised over the term of the arrangement, or an estimate of the economic life of the products offered, beginning with the delivery of the first product.

In addition to the licence fees, contracts generally contain an agreement to provide post contract support (support, maintenance and training) which consists of an identified customer contact at the group and telephonic or e-mail support. Fees for post contract support which take place after customer acceptance are specified in the contract. The fees are determined based on the group's price list as if sold separately. The price list is established and regularly reviewed by management. Revenue for post contract support is recognised on a straight-line basis over the period for which support and maintenance is contractually agreed by the group with the licensee.

Sales of software, including development systems, which are not specifically designed for a given licence (such as off-the-shelf software) are recognised upon delivery. At that time, the group has no further obligations except that, where necessary, the costs associated with providing post contract support have been accrued. Services (such as training) that the group provides which are not essential to the functionality of the IP are separately stated and priced in the contract and, therefore, accounted for separately. Revenue is recognised as services are performed and collectability is probable.

The excess of licence fees invoiced over revenue recognised in respect of such fees is recorded as deferred income.

Royalty revenues are earned on sales by the group's customers of products containing ARM technology. Revenues are recognised when ARM receives notification from the customer of product sales, or receives payment of any fixed royalties, normally quarterly in arrears.

Revenue from consulting is recognised when the service has been provided and all obligations to the customer under the consulting agreement have been fulfilled. For larger consulting projects containing several project milestones, revenue is recognised on a percentage-to-completion basis as milestones are achieved. Consulting costs are recognised when incurred.

As disclosed above, in accordance with FRS 18, "Accounting policies", the group makes significant estimates in applying its revenue recognition policies. In particular, as discussed in detail above, estimates are made in relation to the use of the percentage-to-completion accounting method, which requires that the extent of progress toward completion of contracts may be anticipated with reasonable certainty. The use of the percentage-to-completion method is itself based on the assumption that, at the outset of licence agreements, customer acceptance is not uncertain. In addition, when allocating revenue to various elements of multi-element arrangements, it is assumed that the fair value of each element is reflected by its price when sold separately. The complexity of the estimation process and issues related to the assumptions, risks and uncertainties inherent with the application of the revenue recognition policies affect the amounts reported in the financial statements. If different assumptions were used, it is possible that different amounts would be reported in the financial statements.

Transactions with 'trigger events'

7.9   Occasionally, a contract may contain a 'trigger event' before the performance of which the customer would pay nothing, irrespective of whether or not the customer has received any benefit under the contract to date. Contracts that contain a trigger event expressly depart from the principle that revenue should be recognised as performance occurs, because although performance may have occurred to some extent, the seller and the buyer specifically agree that the seller will not be entitled to revenue until the trigger event occurs. The seller, therefore, should not recognise any revenue, in such situations, until the trigger event occurs, because until that point it is not probable that the economic benefits associated with the transaction will flow to the entity.

Example – trigger event

A professional services company provides advice to a bidder in a take-over situation. Fees are charged on a time basis, but will not be payable unless the bid is declared unconditional. The company normally bills its fees monthly. When should revenue be recognised?

The trigger event here is the bid being declared unconditional. Until that point no revenue should be recognised by the professional services company, even though it may have provided services. This is because until that point revenue is not receivable and if that trigger point is not achieved, no revenue will be received.

Fair values not available for separable components

7.10   The approach described above under 'Transactions involving several components' (see para 7.1 onwards) is often termed 'unbundling' and consists of assigning fair values to the separable components. In some situations, however, it may be possible only to apply the unbundling technique to a part of the contract or not at all. IAS 18 does not deal specifically with such situations, but the ASB's discussion paper, 'Revenue recognition', issued in July 2001 provides guidance that may be useful in applying IAS 18 and proposes that two further techniques may be possible. These are:

■   Value to date assessment.

■   Value outstanding assessment.

7.11   The former of these involves assessing the fair value based on the stage of completion or performance to date, which is then used to determine the extent to which revenue may be recognised. This technique is often used in the construction industry where an independent third party periodically assesses the value of contract work performed.

7.12   Where it is not possible to apply this technique the second of the above methods may be used. This method involves assessing the benefit that has not yet accrued to the customer. In effect this poses the question; if there was no further performance from the seller, what would the customer have to pay a third party to complete the contract?

7.13   This technique is less effective than either unbundling or the value to date assessment. This is because assessing what a third party would charge to take over an incomplete contract may overstate the revenue relating to unperformed activities, because a third party would probably have to duplicate some of the activity already carried out and thus the revenue that should be recognised in the current reporting period may be understated. For this reason, it should only be used where the other two methods are not practicable.

Separate components treated as one transaction to reflect the substance

7.14   IAS 1, 'Presentation of financial statements', requires accounting policies to reflect the economic substance of events and transactions and not merely their legal form. [IAS 1 para 20(b)(ii)]. IAS 18 reflects this by stating that where two or more transactions are linked they should be treated as a single transaction where that is necessary to understand the transaction's commercial effect. It gives as an example the situation where an entity sells goods, but at the same time enters into an agreement to repurchase the goods at a later date, so negating the substantive effect of the original sale. It states that in such a situation the two transactions should be dealt with as one whole transaction. [IAS 18 para 13].

7.15   The standard gives an example in the appendix of such sale and repurchase agreements (other than swap transactions), where the seller concurrently agrees to repurchase the same goods at a later date or when the seller has a call option to repurchase, or the buyer has a put option to require the repurchase, of the goods. In such a situation, the standard states that the agreement's terms need to be analysed to ascertain whether, in substance, the seller has transferred the risks and rewards of ownership to the buyer and whether revenue should, therefore, be recognised. It states that when the seller has retained the risks and rewards of ownership, even though legal title has been transferred, the transaction is a financing and does not give rise to revenue. [IAS 18 App A para 5]. Also, the UK standard FRS 5, 'Reporting the substance of transactions', deals in more detail with such transactions and may provide additional guidance that will be useful in applying the principles of IAS 18.

7.16 Another example would be so-called 'two-way trading transactions'. Sometimes an issue can arise, where one company sells one product to another company and that other company sells a different product to the first company. Provided the two transactions are not connected no problem arises. However, problems may arise where the transactions are connected, for example:

■ Company A may sell a product to company B, which company B uses in the manufacture of a product that is then purchased by company A.

■ A retailer may buy goods from a manufacturer and the manufacturer may pay the retailer to promote those products, for example, by displaying advertising material round its stores.

7.17 In the first of these examples the issue to decide is whether or not the two transactions should be regarded as two separate contracts or together as one larger contract. The latter will be the case if the contracts are legally or economically conditional or dependent on each other, for example, if company A is obliged to purchase the finished product from company B. However, if the contracts are genuinely independent of each other they will be treated as two contracts and company A will recognise profit on the first sale to company B and record the price paid for the product purchased from company B as the cost of that purchase. Generally, the individual circumstances of the arrangements will need to be analysed, but signs that the contracts are independent would include:

- Company B selling the product manufactured from products supplied by company A to other third parties.

- Company A having no obligation to purchase the product from company B.

- Arm's length market prices for each transaction with price risk resting with company B between the first transaction and the second.

7.18 In relation to the second example above, where a supplier pays a retailer to advertise its products and the retailer purchases goods from the supplier, the same principle would apply if the transactions are to be accounted for as separate transactions. That is, the transactions must not be legally or commercially conditional or dependent on each other. This would be so if the prices are arm's length and if the retailer is not obliged to make a certain level of purchases from the supplier in order to obtain the advertising revenue.

7.19 In this second example, if the two transactions are treated as one (possibly because the two conditions detailed above are not met) then it may be necessary to determine whether there is an element of barter, that is goods for advertising (see para 8.1 onwards). In that situation it will be necessary to determine the fair value (market price) to the advertiser of the promotional activity in order to determine:

- the extent, if any, to which promotional activity should be seen as giving rise to service revenue for the retailer; and

- the extent to which the promotional payment should be treated as a reduction in the price of the products bought by the retailer.

7.20 The ASB discussion paper summarises the principle proposed as follows: *"Two contracts should be accounted for separately if they are genuinely independent of one another, but should be treated as one larger contract if, either legally or economically, one is conditional or dependent on the other. Such economic dependence may arise if, for*

buy any doors from that manufacturer. Therefore, the sales and purchases should be accounted for as separate, distinct transactions.

However, if the facts had been different then the accounting might have been different too. For example, if company A sold the materials (which cost it £5) for £10 per profile and at that time agreed to buy back the materials made up into a finished door with glass fitted for £100, then the two transactions would be linked. This is because the sale carries a corresponding commitment to repurchase the materials in the future at a fixed price. For that reason company A should not record a sale of the £10 materials (or a profit on that sale). Instead the cost of the materials should be retained in inventory and the £10 received from the manufacturer should be recorded as a liability. When the door is repurchased the additional net £90 paid by company A will be recorded as inventory, giving an inventory value for the completed door of £95.

7.22 Transactions whereby cash is paid by party A to party B are sometimes related to transactions that require party B to pay cash to party A. These transactions have to be carefully analysed to determine if they should be viewed as separate transactions or a single transaction accounted for on a net basis. Factors to consider (in addition to those outlined above) that might lead to a net presentation include:

■ The arrangements are entered into in close time proximity to each other and/or their mutual existence is acknowledged in the separate agreements.

■ Sufficient verifiable objective evidence does not exist to support the assertion that the amount being charged for the product or service in each transaction is its fair value.

■ The party to the transactions that receives the greater amount of cash inflows does not have a clear immediate business need for the product or service it is purchasing.

7.23 The latter point is even more problematic if the party had received cash before it was obligated to pay cash. These types of transactions can be particularly troublesome if they involve what is, in reality, a barter transaction, such as advertising for advertising which is discussed under 'Exchanges of goods or services and barter transactions' in paragraph 8.1 onwards.

Chapter 8

Exchanges of goods or services and barter transactions

8.1 Companies usually trade for cash or the right to receive cash. Sometimes, however, transactions are undertaken that involve the swapping of goods or services. These are known as barter transactions. IAS 18 does not permit revenue to be recognised in an exchange or barter of similar goods or services. [IAS 18 para 12]. Therefore, the following paragraphs deal only with exchanges of goods or services of a dissimilar nature. (See also paras 6.5 and 6.6 above).

8.2 In terms of determining the point at which a sale should be recognised, the accounting for barter transactions is no different from accounting for transactions that are settled in cash. Measurement of the value of, or consideration for, barter transactions is, however, much more difficult than measurement of the consideration for transactions undertaken for cash or the right to receive cash.

8.3 Where goods or services are exchanged for goods or services of a dissimilar nature, the revenue is measured at the fair value of the goods or services received, adjusted by the amount of any cash or cash equivalents received or paid. If the fair value of the goods or services received cannot be reliably measured, the revenue is measured at the fair value of the goods or services given up, again adjusted by the amount of cash or cash equivalents received. [IAS 18 para 12].

8.4 A particular issue that arose during the 'dotcom' boom of the late nineties, but which is of continuing relevance, is the exchange of advertising services by entities. To deal with the issues SIC 31, 'Revenue – Barter transactions involving advertising services', was issued in May 2001 and became effective on 31 December 2001.

Exchanges of goods or services and barter transactions

8.5   SIC 31 notes that the exchange of similar advertising services does not give rise to revenue under IAS 18 and that it, therefore, deals only with the exchange of dissimilar advertising services. It deals with advertising on the internet, on poster sites, on television or radio, published in magazines or journals or through some other medium.

8.6   The conclusions of SIC 31 are that revenue from an exchange involving advertising services cannot be reliably measured by reference to the fair value of the services received. This is because reliable information is not available to the seller to support such measurement. Therefore, revenue in such circumstances should be measured at the fair value of the services supplied by the selling entity.

8.7   However, SIC 31 then states that the seller can only reliably measure the fair value of advertising services it provides in the exchange by reference to non-barter transactions. For such evidence to be sufficient for reliable measurement the non-barter transactions must:

■   Involve advertising similar to the advertising in the barter transaction.

■   Occur frequently.

■   Represent a predominant number of transactions and amount when compared to all transactions to provide advertising that is similar to the advertising in the barter transaction.

■   Involve cash and/or another form of consideration (for example, marketable securities, non-monetary assets and other services) that has a fair value that is reliably measurable.

■   Not involve the same third party as in the barter transaction.

[SIC 31 para 5].

8.8   An exchange of cheques does not constitute reliable evidence of fair value, but a partial cash payment may provide such evidence to the extent of the cash element, except where partial cash payments are exchanged. Furthermore, a partial cash payment does not provide reliable evidence of the fair value of the entire transaction. [SIC 31 para 9].

8.9   Another issue that arose more recently is that of exchanges of capacity by telecoms companies. No international interpretation has yet been issued on this subject, but the UK UITF has issued Abstract 36, 'Contracts for sales of capacity', in March 2003 that provides useful guidance.

8.10   In relation to exchanges of capacity UITF Abstract 36 takes a similar line to SIC 31 on advertising services. It concludes:

"Turnover or gains in respect of contracts to provide capacity in exchange for receiving capacity should be recognised only if the assets or services provided or received have a readily ascertainable market value. The same principle applies to reciprocal transactions to provide capacity entered into wholly or in part for a cash consideration. No accounting recognition should be given to transactions that are artificial or lacking in substance." [UITF 36 para 23].

For the above purpose 'readily ascertainable market value' means the value of an asset that is established by reference to a market where:

■   the asset belongs to a homogeneous population of assets that are equivalent in all material respects; and

■   an active market, evidenced by frequent transactions, exists for that population of assets.

In view of the similarity of the circumstances and conclusions between UITF Abstract 36 and the SIC we consider that the approach set out in the Abstract should also be used in applying IAS 18 to such transactions.

8.11   The general rules relating to exchanges of goods or services and barter transactions are described above in paragraphs 6.5 and 6.6. The standard also requires disclosure of the amount of revenue recognised in respect of exchange transactions for each major category of revenue (see para 12.2 below).

8.12 Table 4 is an example of a company that discloses its policy on exchanges of advertising and capacity (IRUs).

Table 4 – TeliaSonera AB – Annual Report – 31 December 2002

6 Net Sales (extract)

In the portal operations, ad swapping with another portal provider is not recognized as revenue. Within the international carrier operations, sales of Indefeasible Rights of Use (IRU) regarding fiber and ducts are recognized as revenue over the period of the agreement (see also note "Contractual Obligations and Leasing Agreements"). When entering into swap contracts for infrastructure and capacity with other carriers, evenly balanced swap-deals and the non-cash part of unbalanced swap-deals are not recorded as revenue or expense in the consolidated accounts, as the contracts refer to assets of similar nature and value. Therefore, they are recognized based on the carrying value of the assets exchanged, rather than at fair value. In an unbalanced swap-deal, any cash paid is recorded as an asset and any cash received is recorded as deferred revenue. These amounts are recognized in operations over the term of the related contracts on a straight-line basis. In transactions where the monetary consideration received is at least 25 per cent of the fair value of the exchange, and the fair value of the assets transferred is reasonably determinable, the exchange is treated as part monetary and part non-monetary.

Until both parties have fulfilled all deliveries as agreed, the value provided might differ from the value received. The value of the unfulfilled deliveries in a swap-deal is recorded as a current liability (net received) or a current receivable (net provided). The corresponding asset or deferred revenue is not amortized until delivery has occurred.

28 Leasing Agreements and Contractual Obligations (extract)

TeliaSonera as operating lessor

Fiber and ducts are sold as part of the operations of TeliaSonera's international carrier business.

Exchanges of goods or services and barter transactions

TeliaSonera has decided to view these as integral equipment. Under the agreements, title was not transferred to the lessee. The transactions are therefore recorded as operating lease agreements. Direct expenditures incurred in connection with agreements are capitalized and written off over the term of the agreement. The contracted sale price is chiefly paid in advance and is recognized as revenue during the period of the agreement. Sales not recognized in income are recorded as long-term liabilities and prepaid revenues.

Chapter 9

Options

Options granted for consideration

Options to buy goods or services in the future for which consideration has been received – including joining and membership fees

9.1   IAS 18 does not deal specifically with options to require future performance, but the ASB's discussion paper on revenue recognition proposes that: *"Where a customer pays for an option to require future performance from a seller, that payment gives rise to a liability, which should be released as revenue only when the future performance to which it relates occurs. Because the number of options that will lapse unexercised cannot be known with certainty, the relationship between proceeds and performance should be estimated at the outset and estimates revised over the period of performance."* Treatment of amounts received in advance of performance as a liability is consistent with IAS 18.

9.2   The sale of an option is a transaction with the customer, but needs to be considered together with the further transaction that arises if and when the option is exercised, because the two are inter-dependent. The revenue from the option's sale will generally be accounted for when the seller performs under the further transaction – that is, when the seller supplies the goods or services on exercise of the option.

9.3   In respect of options that have been sold, a certain number may be expected to lapse unexercised. The ASB's discussion paper proposes that there should be no immediate revenue recognised in respect of options that are expected to lapse unexercised. Rather the release of the liability for prepaid options as each option is exercised should be based on the total liability divided by the number of options expected to be exercised.

Options

The number of options expected to be exercised should be estimated at the outset and the estimates should be revised periodically over the performance period, with the rate of release of the liability adjusted accordingly.

Example

A company sells 1,000 options for £5 each, which entitle the option holder to purchase a particular product for £30. The company recognises a liability for unexercised options, initially, of £5,000.

The company estimates at the outset that 80% of the options would be exercised (that is, 20% would lapse unexercised) and, therefore, releases £6.25 (£5,000 divided by 800) instead of £5 (£5,000 divided by 1,000) each time an option is exercised.

Therefore, it records £36.25 per item sold, instead of £35.00 (which it would have recorded if it expected all the options to be exercised).

However, after 500 options have been exercised the company re-estimates that the total number of options that will be exercised will be 900, not 800. At this point there is £1,875 left of the liability for option exercises (£5,000 less 6.25 x 500, that is £3,125). There are 400 more options exercises now expected, so the company should now release £1,875 divided by 400 or £4.69 per options exercise.

If instead, after 500 options had been exercised the company re-estimated that the total number of options that would be exercised was only 600, it would release £18.75 per option exercise (£1,875 divided by 600 less 500).

Membership fees

9.4   A second issue that arises with options issued for consideration is whether it is always possible to determine the extent to which the supplier has performed under the contract. The discussion paper illustrates the issue by considering an option that is not usually described as such – a non-refundable joining fee for a sports club. In effect this is the sale of an option, because it gives the member the right to pay regular membership fees and thereby obtain the rights of access to the club.

9.5   The discussion paper concludes that the non-refundable joining fee should be recognised as income as the club performs by providing access to its premises. However, the problem is in determining what that performance period is, as the member may pay membership fees for one or several years and so the membership period is not known at the outset. The discussion paper proposes that the period of membership should be estimated for members in aggregate at the outset and estimates should be revised over the period of performance. The joining fee would then be spread over this estimated period.

9.6   The ASB's proposed approach contrasts somewhat with the guidance given in the appendix to IAS 18 that deals with initiation, entrance and membership fees. This guidance states that revenue recognition depends on the nature of the services provided. If the fee covers membership, or joining, only and other services or products are paid for separately, or if there is a separate annual subscription, the joining or membership fee is recognised as revenue when there is no significant uncertainty as to its collectability. If the joining or membership fee entitles the member to services or products during the membership period, or to purchase goods or services at prices lower than those charged to non-members, revenue is recognised on a basis that reflects the timing, nature and value of the benefits provided. [IAS 18 App A para 17].

9.7   The issue appears to come down to whether it is possible in any given situation to separate clearly the membership or joining fee from other goods or services that are provided during the membership period. The ASB's approach assumes that the joining fee is inseparable from such goods and services and so should be spread over the expected period of membership. The IAS 18 approach requires an analysis of the arrangement to see whether any part of the joining fee is in fact an advance payment for future goods or services.

9.8 The ASB's approach is the more prudent and less subject to manipulation – for example, by charging substantial up-front fees with future services being provided at reduced prices. However, the IASB's approach has perhaps more regard to the specific circumstances. Both approaches, however, would require that no revenue is recognised up-front if the consideration relates to the provision of future goods and services. Adoption of the more conservative approach in the ASB's discussion paper would be consistent with IAS 18, where it is considered impracticable to ascertain the extent to which the up-front fee is attributable to future services.

Example

An entity that runs a sports-centre charges a joining fee of £250 entitling members to life membership. There are no annual membership charges and members pay £4 per session at the centre. Non-members are allowed to use the centre for £6 per visit. Based on historical records, the entity estimates that members use the centre about 50 times a year and that, on average, each member remains active for 2 years. It asks how it should account for the joining fee. No extra services are provided to members compared to non-members.

The discount that members obtain can be estimated at £200, being the £2 discount for each visit compared to a non-member times the average number of visits (100) made by a member during his or her active membership. Under IAS 18, therefore, £50 may be recognised as revenue when membership commences, but the remaining £200 should be spread over the expected two years of active membership.

If it had not been possible to estimate reliably the discount that would be provided to members in respect of future services, the approach in the ASB's discussion paper (which in that case would be consistent with IAS 18) would be adopted and the whole amount would be spread. If the unknown factor was the period of active membership, the amount would be spread by reference to the expected number of visits; and if the unknown factor was the number of visits, the amount would be spread over the expected period of active membership.

Options granted without consideration

Options to buy goods or services in the future for which consideration has not been received – including money off coupons, two for the price of one etc

9.9 Some options may be granted for no consideration. An example of where an option is granted without consideration is where a supermarket or manufacturer issues money-off coupons or vouchers.

9.10 Such offers may not constitute a legal contract (because a legal contract requires there to be consideration) and instead there may be only a written offer to sell the product at a reduced price. Because the coupons or vouchers do not constitute a contract there will be no obligation on the part of the supermarket or manufacturer to honour them. In practice, however, such offers usually constitute a commercial obligation, because of the reputational damage that would follow if they were not honoured.

9.11 When the money-off coupon or voucher does not result in the supermarket or manufacturer making a loss on the sale of the item, the accounting is the same whether or not there is an obligation. This is because when the transaction occurs there will be a net inflow of economic benefits, which will be recorded at that time. Therefore, there is no obligation or liability to record.

9.12 If, however, the exercise of the coupon or voucher does result in the supermarket or the manufacturer making a loss on the transaction, it would be necessary to consider when the loss should be recognised. If the transaction relates to a particular line of inventory, it may be necessary to write down the carrying value of the inventory to the amount that it is expected to realise, taking account of the expected level of exercise of the coupons or vouchers. If the offer relates to items that are not held in inventory, it would be necessary to decide whether the supermarket or manufacturer had a constructive obligation to honour the coupons/ vouchers. If so and the supermarket or manufacturer becomes obliged to supply goods or services at a loss, it would be necessary to decide whether this amounted to an onerous contract that should be provided for under IAS 37, 'Provisions, contingent liabilities and contingent assets'. It is, however, rather more likely that such an offer would be in the nature of a loss leader, designed to attract customers who would buy other profitable goods at the same time. As such, any losses on these offers would be accounted for as they occurred and would not be provided for as onerous contracts.

9.13 Only if the offers were clearly going to result in losses that would not be offset by other profits would a provision for an onerous contract under IAS 37 be appropriate and this would be expected to be extremely rare (and a sign of a very poor sales strategy).

9.14 Another example of where a provision would be inappropriate is where the money-off coupon or voucher is linked to the purchase of a second item. For example, the money-off coupon or voucher may be usable only on a second item if a first item is purchased at full value. In such a situation, it is more appropriate to treat part of the price of the first item as being the consideration for the 'money-off' coupon. This is consistent with the substance principle in IAS 18 (see also para 7.14 above) that one or more transactions should be considered together when they are linked in such a way that their commercial effect cannot be understood without reference to the series of transactions as a whole. [IAS 18 para 13].

Example

A company buys a particular product at £5 and normally sells it for £8. It gives an offer of 50% off a second item if a customer buys two. How should this be accounted for?

If accounted for separately there is a gain on the first item of £3 (£8–£5) and a loss on the second item of £1 (£4–£5). However, the company should not provide in advance for the losses on the second item. This is because the discount on the second item cannot occur without the profit on the first item. Overall there is a gain of £2 on the transaction (£12–£10) and, therefore, there is no onerous contract or other loss to provide for in advance.

Whether or not part of the consideration from the first sale should be allocated to the sale of the coupon/voucher in this simple example will depend on the materiality of the amounts involved, which in turn may depend on the volume of the transactions. If an allocation were to be done a figure of £2 would probably be appropriate. If that were done the proceeds of the first sale would be £6 and the proceeds of the second sale plus the sale of the voucher would also be £6 (£4 + £2).

9.15 Some sales promotions are described as 'buy one, get one free' or 'two for the price of one', or a vendor may price products below cost to attract volume. Some have argued that the cost of the free product or the negative margin on a 'loss leader' is a marketing expense or that revenues, cost of sales and marketing expense should be grossed-up to reflect the normal selling price of the 'free' product. We do not consider that this argument is appropriate. The revenue is the actual sales proceeds and the purchase or production cost of the 'free' product and 'loss leader' is always a cost of sale. On the other hand, the cost of relatively insignificant promotional give-aways that are not part of the vendor's normal product offerings (for example, a 'free' bookmark with the purchase of a book, or a 'free' T-shirt bearing the logo of the vendor if you purchase £50 of merchandise) might be appropriately classified as a marketing expense.

Points schemes and other similar schemes

9.16 Some companies offer point schemes. Examples are airlines that offer 'free' air miles and supermarkets that offer loyalty cards that amass points that can then be used to reduce the cost of future purchases or may sometimes be redeemable for cash.

9.17 IAS 18 does not deal specifically with points schemes. However, the ASB discussion paper contains an appendix that discusses accounting for point schemes. It suggests that the initial step is to derive a value of points awarded. This should be based on the fair value of the points to the customer, which, for practical purposes, means the fair value of the goods for which the points can be exchanged. It should not be based on the cost to the company of supplying the goods into which the points could be exchanged. This can be used to deduce an 'exchange rate' for each of the goods and services and from that an average exchange rate can be derived. The discussion paper remarks that in effect the points can be thought of as analogous to a foreign currency. The approach in the discussion paper is consistent with the principles of IAS 18, because it results in not recognising revenue before the conditions set out in paragraph 5.2 above have been satisfied. Recognising revenue before the exchange of points for goods has taken place and merely providing for the cost of the goods would not be consistent with the principles of IAS 18.

Example

A company gives away 800 points with each purchase of goods valued at £100. These points can be exchanged for goods, supplied either by the company or by a third party. For every 1,000 points, goods with an average fair value of £5 can be obtained. If the company provides these goods itself its cost is 80p. What is the 'exchange rate' of 100 points?

The exchange rate is 50p being the fair value of goods obtainable for 100 points. It is not 8p as that is the cost to the company of providing the goods. The total consideration received for the original purchase of goods should, therefore, be allocated as to £100 less eight-tenths of £5 (that is, £4) making £96 for the goods and £4 for the points. The £4 should then be treated as deferred revenue (as a liability) until the points are redeemed.

9.18   In some cases the points scheme may be run by a third party on behalf of the selling company and the company makes a payment to the third party in respect of points granted by the third party. In principle this should not alter the way in which the company accounts for the points scheme, but in practice the payments to the third party may be close to the fair value of the points to the customer and it may be more practicable to use the payments to the third party (the operator) as a substitute for the fair value of the points.

9.19 If the agency relationship between the selling company and the operator is disclosed the customer will not have recourse to the selling company for unredeemed points. The selling company's only liability will be to make the necessary payment to the operator and the liability for this will be recorded when the goods that give rise to the points are sold. The selling company's income in respect of the points will not be the consideration received (which it has to pay over to the operator), but instead will be any commission it receives from the principal (the operator).

9.20 If, as is more likely, the agency is undisclosed the revenue from the sale of points will belong to the selling company. However, as noted above in that situation the proceeds will be treated as a liability of the selling company until the points are redeemed. The selling company will also usually have to pay a fee to the operator for providing the service of operating the scheme.

9.21 Other reward schemes that are similar to points schemes are where customers become entitled to benefits (such as free products) when they have satisfied certain criteria. Such criteria might be achieving a certain level of purchases or they might be time based, for example, continuing to be a member of a scheme for a specified period.

9.22 Where benefits are based on achieving a level of purchases the benefit should be recognised by the supplier as the purchases occur. That is part of the revenue equal to the fair value of the benefit to the customer should be deferred. This should be deferred until the free products are given (and matched against any costs thereof which are then charged).

9.23 Where a benefit is given in the form of a cash rebate the payment should be charged against the revenue that has been deferred, so that only the net revenue is recorded. This makes sense because reported revenue should not exceed amounts paid by the customer.

9.24 For those who *receive* rebates or free products on the attainment of certain targets the benefit should not be recognised until the targets are reached and receipt of the benefit is virtually certain.

Options

9.25 Where criteria are based on a time factor, for instance on remaining a member for a specified period, consideration needs to be given as to whether the customer needs to complete any act of performance or whether the criteria are genuinely time based. Criteria that are time based with no act of performance are likely to be extremely rare. Generally, there will be some act of performance such as payment of a membership fee or subscription. In such situations, part of the fee or subscription should be treated as deferred revenue and recognised when the free products or other benefits are claimed (and any other associated costs are recognised). Where the benefits are genuinely time based only with no act of performance required the obligation arises immediately and provision would need to be made (as there is no associated revenue there is no revenue to defer) and discounted if necessary to reflect the fact that the benefit may not be claimable until some later time.

Chapter 10

Agency arrangements

General rules

10.1 The issue concerning agency arrangements is whether the company is functioning as a:

■ Disclosed agent (thereby only reflecting its agency fee or commission revenue in its profit and loss account, that is, product or service revenue and corresponding cost of sale are not reported).

■ Principal (thereby reflecting the full amount paid by the end-user as revenue and the corresponding product or service cost of sale in its profit and loss account).

The decision as to the way in which the entity is functioning is always dependent on the facts and circumstances of the relationship.

10.2 IAS 18 does not deal in detail with agency arrangements, but says *. . .in an agency relationship, the gross inflows of economic benefits include amounts collected on behalf of the principal and which do not result in increases in equity for the enterprise. The amounts collected on behalf of the principal are not revenue. Instead revenue is the amount of commission.* [IAS 18 para 8]. This corresponds to the situation where the agent is a disclosed agent, but does not necessarily cover the more complicated situation where the agency relationship is undisclosed, where the agent may effectively be in the same position as if it were the principal.

10.3 It can sometimes be difficult to determine whether an entity is functioning as an agent or as a principal. At a minimum, a principal has:

- The contractual relationship with the customer, that is, the customer believes he is doing business with the principal (for example, the customer looks to the principal for 'customer satisfaction' issues, such as warranty claims beyond those provided by a third party manufacturer and product returns).

- The ability to set the terms of the transactions (for example, selling price, payment terms, decisions as to extension of credit, etc).

- Whatever inventory risk might exist (for example, loss in value of product carried in inventory or returned is borne by the principal).

- Whatever credit risk might exist (for example, if the customer fails to pay, the principal bears the loss).

- Control over how the physical flow of funds will occur.

- Responsibility for the collection and remission of any sales or similar tax that is imposed on the transaction.

10.4 However, just because those conditions are present does not always mean the entity is functioning as a principal and the transaction should be grossed-up in its profit and loss account. In some situations the risks, while present, may not be substantive.

10.5 The example below illustrates the application of revenue recognition to an agency arrangement involving the distribution of goods.

Example

Entity A distributes entity B's products under a distribution agreement. The terms and conditions of the contract are such that entity A:

- Obtains title to the goods and sells them to third party retailers.

- Stores, repackages, transports and invoices the goods sold to third party retailers.

■ Earns a fixed margin on the products sold to the retailers, but has no flexibility in establishing the sales price.

■ Has the right to return the goods to entity B without penalty.

■ Is responsible for the goods while the goods are stored in entity A's warehouse, but entity B bears the risk of obsolete goods.

Entity B retains product liability. Entity B is, therefore, responsible for manufacturing defects. Also, the credit risk rests with entity B.

(a) Should entity B recognise revenue on the transfer of the goods to entity A?

No, entity B should not recognise revenue on the transfer of the goods to entity A. Entity A is acting as agent for the principal, entity B. Entity B does not transfer the risks and rewards of ownership of the goods to entity A. Entity A has the option to return the goods and entity B bears the product and inventory risks. Entity B retains continuing managerial involvement over the goods by being able to set the sales price. Therefore, entity B should continue to recognise the inventory on its balance sheet and it should only recognise revenue once substantially all the risks and rewards of ownership have been transferred, which will be when entity A sells the goods to a third party.

(b) What revenue should entity A recognise?

Entity A should recognise an agency fee or commission revenue in its income statement.

Advertising agency commissions

10.6 Revenue should only be recognised on transactions including advertising commissions when the service is completed. The income of advertising agencies may consist of media commissions, which relate to the advert appearing before the public and production commissions, which relate to production of the advert. Recognition should occur for media commissions when the advert appears before the public and for production commissions according to the stage of completion of the project. [IAS 18 App A para 12].

Insurance agency commissions

10.7 The appendix to IAS 18 states that insurance agency commissions are recognised on the effective date of commencement or renewal of the related policies, if the agent is not required to render further service. However, where it is probable that the agent will be required to render further services during the life of the policy, the commission or part thereof is deferred and recognised as revenue over the period during which the policy is in force. [IAS 18 App A para 13]. Whether part or all of the commission is deferred in the latter situation will depend on whether separate fair values can be ascertained for the initial and ongoing services such that they may be treated as separate components. In most situations this is probably unlikely.

Chapter 11

Other practical applications

The basic rules for sale of goods

11.1 The principles set out in paragraph 5.2 above are sufficient for the most straightforward of transactions. For example, a contract for the sale of goods will normally give rise to revenue recognition when all the criteria above have been satisfied. That is usually when delivery of the goods to the customer takes place. The example below illustrates the application of the revenue recognition principles and also illustrates how the application of the assets and liabilities approach and the matching concept can give the same result.

Example

In this example various scenarios are set out and the application of the basic principles examined.

Scenario 1
Goods costing £5,000 purchased in year 1 and sold (and delivered) for £8,000, also in year 1.

Scenario 2
Goods costing £5,000 purchased in year 1, sold (and delivered) in year 2 for £8,000.

Scenario 3
Goods costing £5,000 purchased in year 1, customer orders goods in year 2 and pays £2,000 in advance, delivery in year 3 with balance of £6,000 paid by customer in that year.

In each scenario the conditions in IAS 18 for recognition of revenue are assumed in the example to have been fulfilled on delivery of the goods.

Revenue recognition would be as follows

Scenario 1
There is a contract for sale in year 1 and the conditions for recognition of revenue are fulfilled in year 1 on delivery of the goods. Therefore, revenue of £8,000 is recognised. At the end of the year, the £5,000 spent on purchasing the goods does not qualify as an asset as it does not give rights to future economic benefits (as those benefits have already been received in the form of the sale consideration). Therefore, the £5,000 is written off to profit and loss as a cost of sale. In this way 'matching' is also achieved.

Scenario 2
At the end of year 1 there is no contract for sale (or sale transaction) so there is no revenue recognised. The cost of the goods (£5,000) qualifies as an asset, because it provides a right or other access to future economic benefit controlled by the entity as a result of a past transaction. Therefore, £5,000 is recorded as an asset – inventory.

In year 2 revenue of £8,000 is recognised as there is a contract for sale and the conditions for recognising revenue are fulfilled on delivery. At the same time the asset of inventory is de-recognised, because there are no longer any future economic benefits to be derived from it and the £5,000 is charged as a cost of sale. Thus 'matching' is achieved in year 2.

Scenario 3
At the end of year 1 there is no contract for sale (or sale transaction) so no revenue is recognised. The cost of the goods (£5,000) qualifies as an asset, because it provides a right or other access to future economic benefits controlled by the entity as a result of a past transaction. Therefore, £5,000 is recorded as an asset – inventory.

In year 2 an order for the inventory is received, so there is a contract. However, because the conditions for recognition of revenue (the example assumes they are only met on delivery) have not been met by the end of year 2 no revenue can be recognised. The customer has, however, paid

£2,000 in advance. This amount should be recorded as a liability until such time as it is discharged (by delivery of the goods) and this applies whether or not the amount is refundable.

In year 3, delivery has occurred and revenue of £8,000 is recognised (£2,000 is released from liabilities and £6,000 is received in the year). The asset of £5,000 is derecognised, because there are no longer any future economic benefits to be derived from it and the £5,000 is charged as a cost of sale. 'Matching' is thus achieved in year 3.

Payments in advance of sale of goods

11.2   It can be difficult to determine when the entity has transferred to the buyer the significant risks and rewards of ownership and retains no further involvement or control of the goods. Payments received in advance of performance do not represent revenue, because they have not been earned. Until the selling entity performs, the increase in cash is matched by an increase in liabilities, such as an obligation to supply goods or services or to make a refund.

Example

A company manufactures and supplies reproduction furniture. Since the choice of the final colouring and polishing of the furniture is left to the customer, the company takes a large non-refundable deposit from the customer at the time of the initial order. In some situations the piece ordered is in stock and only needs finishing before it can be shipped to the customer, in other cases the item needs to be completely manufactured.

There are obviously many points along the production process at which revenue could be recognised:

■   At the initial order and deposit regardless of whether the furniture is in stock.

■   When the deposit is received provided the item only needs to be polished.

■   Only when the goods have been shipped to the customer and the invoice has been raised.

However, the appendix to IAS 18 specifically states that revenue must not be recognised when there is simply an intention to acquire or manufacture the goods in time for delivery. In this case it is not enough to have received payment. It cannot be considered to be earned until the manufacturing process is complete, including the finishing, since this is a significant part of the manufacturing technique. Recognition may need to be delayed until the customer has accepted the goods if the conditions of sale allow the customer to return furniture if the final colour and polish are unsatisfactory and the incidence of such returns cannot be assessed and provided for. If acceptance is unlikely to cause difficulty, then revenue can be recognised on despatch of the completed items.

Goods on sale or return or on consignment

11.3   Paragraphs 5.16 and 5.17 above discuss the accounting principles for the supply of goods on a 'sale or return' basis in straightforward situations. In relation to goods sold on approval or on a sale or return basis, IAS 18 states that if there is uncertainty about the possibility of return, revenue is recognised when the shipment has been formally accepted by the buyer or the goods have been delivered and the time period for rejection has expired. [IAS 18 App A para 2(b)]. Consignment sales or items shipped on a sale or return basis are also covered by the principle of ensuring that performance must have taken place before recognising revenue. If the purchaser of goods on consignment has undertaken to sell the items on behalf of the seller, then revenue should not be recognised by the seller until the purchaser has sold the goods to a third party. [IAS 18 App A para 2(c)]. This recognition point is the same for goods sold on a sale or return basis or sales to distributors or dealers where the purchaser is merely acting as an agent for the seller. [IAS 18 App A para 6].

Example

A company imports sports clothing and has a number of distributors in the UK. It gives its distributors an extended credit deal whereby it supplies new fashion items worth £10,000 to each distributor, which can be sold on to third parties in order to encourage a market in these new items. The distributor does not have to pay for the goods until he has received the payment from the third party to which they are sold. If they are not sold within six months of receipt, the distributor can either return them to the company or pay for them and keep them.

In this situation, revenue should not be recognised by the company until the earlier of the distributor receiving payment for his sale of the goods to a third party or six months after the distributor receives them, provided that they are not returned. It is only at this point that the company can determine whether performance under the sales contract has occurred and the risks and rewards of ownership have passed to the distributor, because until then the goods may be returned to the company. Until it is known whether the goods have been sold, the goods should continue to be treated as the company's inventory.

Goods sold subject to installation and inspection

11.4 IAS 18 states that revenue relating to goods that are sold subject to installation and inspection is normally recognised when the buyer accepts delivery and the installation and inspection are complete. However, revenue is recognised on delivery when:

- The installation process is simple – the standard gives the example of a television receiver where the installation merely requires that the equipment be plugged in and the aerial connected.

- The inspection is performed only for the purpose of determining the contract prices – the standard gives the examples of shipments of iron ore, sugar or soya beans.

[IAS 18 App A para 2(a)].

Installation fees

11.5 IAS 18 states that installation fees are recognised as revenue by reference to the stage of the installation's completion, unless they are incidental to the product's sale in which case they are recognised when the goods are sold. [IAS 18 App A para 10].

11.6 Determining whether installation is incidental or not to the sale of a product is often difficult. In the case of a telephone line, for example, it can be argued that the installation is usually straightforward. Moreover, it is usually charged separately from the line rental.

11.7 Where installation is more complicated, for example, in a contract to supply a computer system, revenue is recognised according to the stage of completion of the whole contract. Alternatively, the contract may be broken down into separate components one of which would be the installation. However, this approach would only be possible where a reliable fair value could be ascertained for the installation component – see paragraph 7.1.

Bill and hold sales

11.8 Bill and hold sales are those where a customer obtains title to goods, but requests that the goods are not delivered immediately but are held by the supplier until the customer requests delivery or collects them.

11.9 Normally, revenue on sale of goods is only recognised when the performance conditions have been satisfied (see para 5.2). One such performance condition is usually delivery of the goods to the buyer.

11.10 The issue, therefore, arises as to whether, in the absence of delivery, revenue can be recognised in a bill and hold sale.

11.11 The response would appear to depend on whether or not there has been substantive performance of the contractual promises. Normally, for example, a customer might make an order for goods and then take delivery. Revenue would be recognised at that point. However, if the supplier agreed to offer a discount to the customer to accept title to the goods before delivery and to request a delay in delivery, the arrangement's substance has not changed, but it could be argued that the arrangement is now a 'bill and hold' sale.

11.12 Clearly, it would be wrong to advance income recognition as the result of an artificial arrangement such as that described above. Therefore, some specific conditions are needed to distinguish bill and hold sales from mere executory contracts. These conditions are:

- The buyer must have taken title to the goods and accepted billing.

- It must be probable that delivery will take place.

- The goods must be on hand, identified and be ready for delivery to the buyer at the time the sale is recognised.

- The buyer must specifically acknowledge the deferred delivery instructions.

- The usual payment terms must apply.

[IAS 18 App A para 1].

11.13 Revenue is not recognised when there is simply an intention to acquire or manufacture the goods in time for delivery. [IAS 18 App A para 1].

11.14 Normally, for goods not subject to a bill and hold arrangement, the passing of economic benefits occurs on delivery, when specific goods are appropriated to the contract and passed to the customer. Until then if the goods are of a general sort manufactured by the seller, the goods are not specific or 'identified'. The seller can still sell inventory that may have been earmarked for the customer and substitute similar inventory when it comes to delivery. Only in the following circumstances should the customer be deemed to have secured the economic benefits of that inventory on passing of title:

- The goods are so specific to the customer that they are unable to be replaced. Examples of such inventory might be stationery that is printed with the name of the customer or goods that have been manufactured to a customer's specification and not otherwise made by the seller or obtainable by the seller from other sources.

- If the inventory is not unique in the way described above the customer must have secured the inventory's economic benefits by transfer of title and must be able to control those benefits through access. This will only be the case when the customer is able to obtain access to the goods without any significant restrictions on that access. Significant restrictions would apply, for example, if access could not be obtained before a certain date. In addition, the seller must be unable to use the inventory for sale to someone else.

Example

Entity A entered into a contract during 20X2 to supply video game consoles to customer B. The contract is for 100,000 game consoles at £50 each. The contract contains specific instructions from customer B with regard to the timing and location of the delivery. Entity A must deliver the consoles to customer B in 20X3 at a date to be specified by the customer. Usual payment terms apply.

At its year end of 31 December 20X2, entity A has inventory of 120,000 game consoles, including the 100,000 relating to the contract with customer B. However, entity A cannot use the 100,000 game consoles to satisfy other sales orders and at 31 December 20X2 title to the 100,000 consoles has passed to customer B. Delivery is expected to take place in 2003. When should entity A recognise revenue?

Considering the criteria in IAS 18 for recognition of revenue in a bill and hold sale at 31 December 20X2:

- Delivery has been delayed at the buyer's request. – Yes, customer B has specified delivery in 2003 in the contract.

- The buyer has taken title. – Yes.

- It is probable that delivery will be made. – Yes.

- The item is on hand, identified and ready for delivery and cannot be used to satisfy other orders. – Yes.

- The buyer specifically acknowledges in writing the deferred delivery instructions. – Yes, this is acknowledged in the contract.

- The seller's usual payment terms apply. – Yes.

In addition, the condition in the second bullet point in the preceding paragraph is met because the customer is able to obtain access to the goods without any significant restrictions on that access. This is because entity A must deliver the consoles at a date to be specified by the customer. The fact that the customer has specified delivery in 2003 does not affect this, as it could have specified a date in 2002.

Therefore, the conditions for revenue recognition have been met in the year to 31 December 20X2 and entity A can recognise 100,000 game consoles as sold.

Lay away sales

11.15 The appendix to IAS 18 considers the situation where goods are delivered only when the buyer makes the final payment in a series of instalments. It states that revenue from such sales is recognised when the goods are delivered. However, where experience indicates that most such sales are completed, revenue may be recognised when a significant deposit is received, provided that the goods are on hand, identified and ready for delivery to the buyer. [IAS 18 App A para 3]. It may in fact be difficult to distinguish this type of sale from a bill and hold sale (see from para 11.8). In any event, one further condition that we consider should be met before revenue can be recognised is that the seller must not be able to dispose of the goods to any party other than that buyer.

Example

Entity A enters into a sale agreement (lay away) to sell 10 television sets at a total price of £15,000 (£1,500 per television) to a customer. Entity A has only five televisions in stock and sets them aside in its inventory. Entity A collects a cash deposit of £1,000 from the customer. The television sets are not released to the customer until the full purchase price is paid. The customer has to finalise the purchase in three months or it forfeits the cash deposit. Entity A must either refund the cash deposit to the customer or provide a replacement product if the television sets are damaged or lost prior to delivery. When should revenue be recognised?

Entity A retains the risk of ownership of the television sets held in inventory until they are delivered to the customer. Also, entity A does not have an enforceable right to the remainder of the purchase price prior to delivery as only the cash deposit is forfeited if the purchase is not finalised. Furthermore all the goods are not on hand, identified and ready for delivery and there is no restriction on entity A selling the goods to another party.

Therefore, entity A should recognise £15,000 as revenue only when the 10 television sets are delivered to the customer. The amount of a cash deposit should be recognised as a liability up to that point.

Sale of property

11.16 IAS 18 states that revenue from sale of property is normally recognised when legal title passes to the buyer. However, as mentioned in paragraph 5.13 above the standard goes on to say that in some jurisdictions the equitable interest may pass before legal title passes. In such circumstances, provided that the seller has no further substantial acts to complete under the contract it may be appropriate to recognise revenue. This is the case in the UK and usually revenue is recognised when there is an unconditional and irrevocable contract for sale. The standard notes that where the seller has any significant acts to perform after the transfer of equitable or legal title, revenue is recognised as the acts are performed. It gives as an example a building or other facility on which construction has not been completed. [IAS 18 App A para 9].

11.17 Transactions involving the sale of property often straddle a financial year end. For example, a contract may be exchanged before the year end and completed after the year end. The legal documentation surrounding the sale should clarify when rights to the property are transferred and legal advice may be necessary in specific situations. In general, however, where an unconditional and irrevocable contract has been entered into for a property's sale, the revenue arising on the sale can be recognised at the time the contract is exchanged.

11.18 It is appropriate to recognise the income when an unconditional and irrevocable contract has been entered into, because the equitable and the beneficial interests already vest in the purchaser, who has a legal commitment for the outstanding purchase consideration. The situation is, therefore, no different from goods sold on credit. If, however, the contract is conditional, recognition should be delayed until the last material condition is satisfied. It is only when all the material conditions have been satisfied that the gain can be considered to be earned. This is illustrated in the example in paragraph 5.45 where the receipt of consideration depends on whether or not the buyer can obtain funding, in which case recognition of the sale is delayed until that uncertainty is removed.

11.19 Property is often sold subject to planning consent being obtained. In these situations, the vendor may be involved in obtaining the required planning consent and may incur costs in submitting planning applications and attending planning hearings. Obtaining the required planning permission is a material condition of the contract. Therefore, even if the vendor has performed all the tasks necessary to obtain consent before the year end, the sale cannot be recognised until the condition is satisfied and the consent has been granted. If such consent is received after the year end, then the sale should be recognised the following year when that material condition has been fulfilled.

11.20 Many companies do not take credit for sales, commonly of private houses, until legal completion has taken place. This policy is, therefore, more conservative than recognising revenue on the exchange of unconditional contracts. The property industry has historically taken a more prudent approach to the sale of homes to individual buyers. However, the choice of either of these methods will usually depend on the circumstances of the sale.

11.21 Therefore, revenue should only be recognised on property sales in a year if a binding and unconditional contract has been entered into before the year end or if the last material condition on a conditional contract has been satisfied before the year end. If the contract is entered into after the year end or if a condition is only fulfilled after the year end, then that sale represents the next year's revenue since it is only in the following year that it has been earned.

11.22 Some property companies enter into transactions in which they build developments for particular customers rather than building speculative developments. The properties built may be effectively pre-sold so that the contract has been entered into before construction begins and all the terms and conditions of the sale are known. In such situations, the transaction may effectively be a construction contract, which should be accounted for in accordance with IAS 11 with profit being recognised according to the development's percentage of completion, provided that the outcome can be assessed with reasonable certainty.

11.23 IAS 18 notes that sometimes property is sold with a degree of continuing involvement by the seller such that the risks and rewards of ownership have not been transferred. An example is a sale with a repurchase agreement which includes put and call options, an agreement whereby the seller guarantees the property's occupancy for a specified period or guarantees a return on the buyer's investment for a specified period. In such situations, the nature and extent of the buyer's involvement determines how the transaction is accounted for. The standard notes that it may be accounted for as a sale or a financing, leasing or some other profit sharing arrangement. It also notes that if accounted for as a sale the continued involvement of the seller may delay revenue recognition. [IAS 18 App A para 9].

11.24 In all situations such as those mentioned above, the transaction's substance should be determined by looking at the transaction or series of transactions as a whole to determine their true commercial effect. IAS 18 requires this by stating that where two or more transactions are linked they should be treated as a single transaction where that is necessary to understand the commercial effect of the transactions (see para 7.14 above). [IAS 18 para 13].

Example

Entity A owns a hotel resort. The resort includes a casino that is housed in a separate building that is part of the premises of the entire hotel resort. The casino's patrons are largely tourists and non-resident visitors. Entity A operates the hotel and other facilities on the hotel resort, including the casino. During the year, the casino was sold to entity B.

A and B agree that A will operate the casino for its remaining useful life. Entity A will receive 85% of the net profit of the casino as operator fees and the remaining 15% will be paid to entity B. Entity A has also provided a guarantee to entity B that the casino will have net profits of at least 10 million. How should revenue be recognised?

Entity A should not recognise the arrangement as a sale of the casino as it continues to enjoy substantially all of the casino's risks and rewards and has a continuing involvement in the casino's management. The transaction is in substance a financing arrangement and the proceeds should be recognised as a borrowing.

11.25 IAS 18 also states that a seller should consider the means of payment and the evidence of the buyer's commitment to complete payment. It notes that when a buyer's initial deposit or continuing payments by the buyer provide insufficient evidence of the buyer's commitment to complete payment, revenue is recognised only to the extent that cash is received. [IAS 18 App A para 9]. It is not entirely clear why the standard makes this point again specifically with respect to property sales. The point is already implicit in the need for probability that the economic benefits will flow to the entity before revenue may be recognised, as discussed in paragraph 5.45 above. It may be that property sales are generally very significant and, therefore, the risk of non-payment is greater than in, for example, retail sales. The example in paragraph 5.45 above illustrates such a situation.

Sale of software

11.26 In the software industry, revenue recognition poses a number of problems, which combine elements of sale of goods and sale of services. Software houses normally earn their revenue from three principal sources:

■ Sale of off-the-shelf or ready made software where the licensing arrangement gives the customer the right to use the software for a specified period.

■ Sale of customised software developed for specific application by the customer.

■ Sale of software support services related to either own software or customised software.

11.27 Selling software is different from selling a tangible product since what is being sold is the right to use a piece of intellectual property rather than the actual computer disk or other media on which the programme is held. The actual delivery of the product in the form of the computer disk may, therefore, appear to be less important than it is where other types of goods are sold. On the other hand, if there is any risk that the customer may reject the software and the product is sold subject to customer satisfaction, then recognition may need to be delayed until after delivery and acceptance by the customer. For example, an off-the-shelf package may require tailoring to meet the customer's specifications. In this situation, if the supply does not qualify as a long-term contract, revenue may not be earned until after delivery, set up and the subsequent testing and acceptance of the software by the customer.

11.28 The sale of a completely standard package such as a word processor package or spreadsheet may need to be treated differently from software that needs to be individually tailored for each customer. Companies that sell standard off-the-shelf packages generally treat their sales no differently from the sale of a physical product and recognise revenue on delivery. An example is Table 5. This is a company that reports under UK GAAP, but its policy is consistent with IAS 18.

Table 5 – Merant plc – Annual Report – 30 April 2002

NOTES TO THE FINANCIAL STATEMENTS (extract)

Licence fees: the Company's standard end user licence agreement for the Company's products provides for an initial fee to use the product in perpetuity up to a maximum number of users. The Company also enters into other types of licence agreement, typically with major end user customers, which allow for the use of the Company's products, usually restricted by the number of employees, the number of users, or the licence term. Licence fees are recognised as revenue upon product shipment, provided a signed agreement is in place, fees are fixed or determinable, no significant vendor obligations remain and collection of the resulting debt is deemed probable. Fees from licences sold together with consulting services are generally recognised upon shipment provided that the above criteria have been met and payment of the licence fees is not dependent upon the performance of the consulting services. Where these criteria have not been met, both the licence and consulting fees are recognised under the percentage of completion method of contract accounting.

Maintenance subscriptions: maintenance agreements generally call for the Company to provide technical support and software updates to customers. Revenue on technical support and software update rights is recognized over the term of the support agreement on a pro-rata basis. Payments for maintenance fees are generally made in advance and are non refundable.

Training and consulting: the Company recognises revenues from consulting and education as the services are performed.

11.29 Where a product is sold subject to continuing obligations under the agreement or the provision of updates free of charge, it will be necessary to determine whether the contract can be broken down into separable components. If it can, revenue will be recognised as the separable components are performed – see above discussion under 'Transactions involving several components' (para 7.1 onwards). Where acceptance of a product is in doubt revenue should be delayed until acceptance.

Example

A company sells software packages, which may be modified to meet the customer's exact requirements. The sequence of the transaction is: order; invoice and delivery; and acceptance by the customer. The order, invoice and delivery may be before the year end, but the acceptance may be after the year end.

Where acceptance is subject to installation and inspection the following rules may be relevant. If the installation process is simple in nature – the example given in IAS 18 is that of installing a factory tested television receiver which only needs to be unpacked and connected – then it is acceptable to recognise revenue immediately upon the buyer's acceptance of delivery. In general, though, recognition should be delayed until the installation and inspection processes are complete. For many types of software packages it is acceptable to recognise revenue when delivery has taken place by the year end. However, when there is a risk that the customer may not accept the package, sufficient evidence must be obtained of the acceptance before revenue can be recognised. Unlike television receivers, software bears more risk of customer rejection and, therefore, acceptance is required to give the necessary assurance of a completed sale.

11.30 The creation of software specifically developed for use by a customer normally requires executing a number of separate acts over a period of time. The product has to be designed and developed according to the customer's specification, adequately tested and finally installed on the customer's hardware. Where a contractual obligation is performed by an indeterminate number of acts over a period of time, revenue should normally be recognised by reference to the developer's stage of completion, in accordance with the principles outlined in IAS 11. Consequently, the software house should recognise revenue in a manner appropriate to the contract's stage of completion, including completion of services provided for post delivery service support, provided that the outcome can be assessed with reasonable certainty. [IAS 18 App A para 19].

11.31 The procedure to recognise profit is to include an appropriate proportion of total contract value as revenue in the profit and loss account as the contract activity progresses. The costs incurred in reaching that stage of completion should be matched with this revenue, resulting in the reporting of results that can be attributed to the proportion of work completed. Where, however, the outcome cannot be assessed with reasonable certainty before the contract's conclusion, or where the contract is of a relatively short duration, the completed contracts method should be applied and, accordingly, revenue should be recognised when final completion takes place.

11.32 When the project involves the provision of hardware as well as software, the contract will need to be carefully reviewed to ensure that income is not recognised before it is earned.

Example

A company is developing a computer system for a customer. It has sold the hardware to the customer for a profit and this has been installed on the site where it will be eventually used, but the company is still working on developing the necessary software. The customer has the right to return the hardware if the software does not work. The company does not anticipate any problems with the software development, which should take about 12 months.

It seems that there is one contract for the supply of both hardware and software. If this is the case, then the treatment in IAS 11 should be followed. Under IAS 11, profit would be required to be taken before the contract's completion, provided that the outcome can be assessed with reasonable certainty. The extent of profit recognition will depend on the degree of certainty over the contract's outcome and on the forecast of the contract's overall performance rather than the margin on the hardware in isolation. If the outcome of the project cannot be assessed with reasonable certainty, then no profit should be reflected in the profit and loss account. If the costs of creating software of the required standard cannot be assessed with reasonable certainty, it is appropriate to delay recognition of the sale.

Even if the contract for the hardware supply could be separated from the software supply there would still be an argument for delaying recognition of the hardware sale. This is because if there is uncertainty about the possibility of return, revenue should only be recognised when the goods have been formally accepted by the customer or the goods have been delivered and the time allowed for their possible rejection has passed. Therefore, until the software has been installed and tested to the customer's satisfaction, revenue should not be recognised and any payments received for the hardware should be included in the financial statements as a liability.

11.33 Where a software house provides maintenance services or other after sales support, it is necessary to determine if this can be regarded as a separable component. If it can (see from para 7.1 above) then revenue under the separable component method is recognised as performance occurs. For example, maintenance revenue will be recognised as the service is provided. See Tables 3 and 5.

Franchise fees

11.34 Franchise agreements may provide for the supply of initial services such as training and assistance to help the franchisee set up and operate the franchise operation, subsequent services and the supply of equipment, inventory and other tangible assets and know-how. Therefore, these agreements may generate different types of revenue such as initial franchise fees, profits and losses from the sale of fixed assets and royalties.

11.35 In general, franchise fees should be recognised on a basis that reflects the purpose for which they were charged. The appendix to IAS 18 states that revenue from the supply of assets should be recognised when the items are delivered or title passes. Fees charged for the use of continuing rights granted by a franchise agreement or for other continuing services provided during the agreement's term should be recognised as the service is provided or the rights are used. [IAS 18 App A para 18].

11.36 However, the appendix to IAS 18 goes on to require that where the franchise agreement provides for the franchisor to supply equipment, inventory or other assets at a price lower than that charged to others, or at a price that does not allow the franchisor to make a reasonable profit on the supplies, part of the initial franchise fee should be deferred. The amount of the initial franchise fee deferred should be sufficient to cover the estimated costs in excess of the price charged to the franchisee for any assets and to allow the franchisor to make a reasonable profit on these sales. This deferred income can then be recognised over the period the goods are likely to be provided. The balance of the initial fee should be recognised when performance of the initial services and other obligations (such as assistance with site selection, staff training, financing and advertising) has been substantially accomplished. This approach is based on the fact that the initial fee in these circumstances is unlikely to be capable of being treated as a separable component.

11.37 Similarly, if there is no separate fee for the supply of continuing services after the initial fee or if the separate fee is not sufficient to cover the cost of providing any subsequent services together with a reasonable profit, then part of the initial fee should also be deferred and recognised as the subsequent services are provided.

11.38 The initial services and other obligations under an area franchise may be based on the number of outlets established in the area. If so, revenue from franchise fees attributable to the initial services is recognised in proportion to the number of outlets for which the initial services have been substantially completed. [IAS 18 App A para 18].

11.39 If the initial fee is collectable over an extended period and there is significant uncertainty as to whether it will be collected in full, revenue should be recognised as collection of the fee is made.

Licensing agreements and royalties

11.40 Royalties include other fees for the use of assets such as trademarks, patents, software, copyright, record masters, films and TV programmes. As noted in paragraph 5.31 above, IAS 18 requires that royalties should be recognised on an accruals basis in accordance with the substance of the relevant agreement. [IAS 18 para 30]. The terms of an agreement will normally indicate when the revenue has been earned. In general, revenue is normally recognised on a straight-line basis over the life of the agreement or another systematic basis such as in relation to sales to which the royalty relates.

11.41 In general, revenue should not be recognised under licensing agreements until the critical event has occurred, that is, performance under the contract has occurred and it has been earned.

Example

A film distributor grants a licence to a cinema operator. The licence entitles the cinema to show the film once for consideration of the higher of a non-refundable guarantee or a percentage of the box office receipts.

The film distributor should recognise the revenue on the date the film is shown. It is usual industry practice for the recognition of both the guaranteed minimum amount and any percentage of box office receipts to be delayed until the exhibition of the film. It is only when the film is shown that the revenue has been earned. (See also Table 6 below for an example of an accounting policy for film distribution.)

11.42 An assignment of rights for a non-refundable amount under a non-cancellable contract that permits the licensee to use those rights freely and where the licensor has no remaining obligations to perform is, in substance, a sale. [IAS 18 App A para 20].

Example

A computer games software house grants two different licences to arcade games machine manufacturers to use the software for a certain game. The annual licence, which has a fee of £100,000, allows the software to be used for one year and can be renewed annually. The perpetual licence, which has a fee of £400,000, allows the software to be used indefinitely with the licensee entitled to upgrades free of charge, although the software house is under no obligation to upgrade the software and does not expect to incur significant costs in performing any upgrades.

Under the perpetual licence there may be a commercial or at least a moral obligation to upgrade the software and there is some cost in doing so. This is also supported by the fact that the perpetual licence costs more than the annual licence. In this situation, there is a strong argument for spreading the licence fee over the expected life of the game in order to match it with the costs of providing the upgrades. The annual licence fee, on the other hand, does not carry any further obligations on the part of the software house and may, therefore, be recognised immediately.

11.43 Another example where a licensing agreement may be recognised as an outright sale is if a non-refundable one-off fee has been received for the foreign exhibition rights to a film that allow the licensee to use the rights at any time in certain countries without restriction. In such a situation, it may be appropriate to recognise the income when the fee is received. Since the licensor has no control over any further use or distribution of the product and has no further action to perform under the contract the licensor has effectively sold the rights detailed in the licensing agreement.

11.44 An example of accounting policies for film and television distribution licences is Table 6.

Table 6 – Senator AG – Annual Report – 31 December 2001

Presentation of accounting and valuation methods (extract)

4.12. Revenue recognition Revenues are recognized in accordance IAS 18 when all of the following conditions have been satisfied:

(a)   Senator AG has transferred to the buyer the significant risks and rewards of ownership of the goods;

(b)   Senator AG retains neither continuing managerial involvement to the degree usually associated with ownership nor effective control over goods sold;

(c)   The amount of revenue can be measured reliably;

(d)   It is sufficiently probable that the economic benefits of the sale will accrue to the company;

(e)   The costs incurred or to be incurred in respect of the transaction can be measured reliably.

Revenues are recorded when the transfer of the risks and rewards of ownership coincides with the transfer of the legal title and the passing of possession to the buyer. If the company retains significant risks of ownership, the transaction revenue is not recognized.

In accordance with the matching principle in IAS 18 revenue and expenses that relate to the same transaction or other event are recognized simultaneously.

(1) Films licensed to cinemas Motion picture exhibition rights are sold (licensed) to theaters on the basis of a percentage of the box office receipts and/or for a flat fee. In certain instances, the Senator AG receives a nonrefundable guarantee against a percentage of the box office receipts.

Senator AG recognizes revenues on the dates of exhibition for both percentage and flat fee engagements.

Nonrefundable guarantees are deferred in the accounts and recognized as revenues on the dates of exhibition. Guarantees that are, in substance, outright sales, are recognized as revenue under certain conditions, as is the case for licensing of TV rights. This also applies to the sale of film rights to other distributors in certain territories.

(2) Films licensed to television Senator AG considers license agreements for television program material as a sale of a right or a group of rights.

Senator AG recognizes revenues from a license agreement for television program material when all of the following conditions have been met:

(a)   The license fee for each film is known;

(b)   The cost of each film is known or reasonably determinable;

(c)   Collectability of the full license fee is reasonably assured;

(d)   The film has been accepted by the licensee in accordance with the conditions of the license agreement;

(e)   The film is available for its first showing or telecast. Unless a conflicting license prevents usage by the licensee, restrictions under the same license agreement or another license agreement with the same licensee on the timing of subsequent showings shall not affect this condition.

Subscriptions to publications and similar items

11.45 In respect of subscriptions and similar items, IAS 18 states that revenue should be recognised on a straight-line basis over the period when the items are despatched, if they are of a similar nature in each time period, such as a typical magazine subscription. Where the items vary in value from one period to another, such as a wine of the month club, revenue is recognised on the basis of the sales value of the item despatched compared to the total estimated sales value of the items covered by the subscription. [IAS 18 App A para 7].

Admission fees

11.46 Joining and membership fees are discussed above under 'Options granted for consideration' (see para 9.1 onwards). Other admission fees from, for example, artistic performances, banquets and other special events are recognised when the event takes place. When a subscription to a number of events is sold the fee is allocated to each event on a basis that reflects the extent to which services are performed at each event. [IAS 18 App A para 15].

11.47 When an event is held at a particular time, income and costs may be received and incurred in advance. For example, exhibitions and conferences or courses may involve delegates paying in advance of attending and certain of the costs, such as advertising, may also be incurred in advance. Since performance does not occur and revenue is thus not earned until the exhibition is held or the course is given, the payments received in advance represent a liability, which can be released to the profit and loss account when the event takes place. A stringent review of the costs incurred before the event is necessary, since such costs should only be carried forward if they are directly related costs and they qualify for recognition as an asset under the Framework.

Tuition fees

11.48 The standard deals briefly with tuition fees, which should be recognised as revenue over the period of instruction. [IAS 18 App A para 16].

11.49 Whilst this deals with the straightforward situation for a course where a single session of tuition is given over a fixed time period, some instruction courses are structured differently. For example, a course may be structured as a number of modules for each of which repeated tuition sessions are staged at regular intervals and the student may choose to attend and complete a module at any time within say a two-year period. In such a situation it would be more appropriate to recognise revenue in proportion to the modules attended and completed by the student, that is, as the service is provided to the student.

Interest and financial service fees

11.50 As mentioned in paragraph 5.4, IAS 18 states that revenues arising from others using an entity's resources, which yield interest, royalties and dividends, should only be recognised when it is probable that the economic benefits associated with the transaction will flow to the entity and the amount of the revenue can be measured reliably. Interest revenue is recognised on a time proportion basis taking account of the effective yield on the asset. [IAS 18 para 30].

11.51 In many situations, the actual rate of interest charged by a lender will be the same as the effective rate (that is, the rate required to discount the expected future income streams over the life of the loan to its initial carrying amount). Other transactions may include elements both of interest and of other financial service fees. For these transactions it is necessary to differentiate between fees that are part of the financial instrument's effective yield and fees that are earned for performing a certain act.

11.52 The appendix to IAS 18 gives guidance on accounting for different types of financial service fees. Reviewing the borrower's credit rating or registering charges, for example, are necessary and integral parts of the lending process. Fees for performing such services should be deferred and recognised as an adjustment to the effective yield. Commitment fees that are charged by the lender when it is probable that a specific transaction will take place should similarly be included in the effective yield, but if the commitment expires without the transaction taking place, then the fee may be recognised as revenue on expiration.

11.53 Other types of financial service fees are earned as the service is provided. For example, commitment fees that are charged by a lender when it is unlikely that a lending arrangement will be entered into should be recognised on a time-apportioned basis over the commitment period. Fees for servicing a loan should also be recognised as the service is provided.

11.54 A third type of financial service fee relates to performing a particular, significant act. Commissions received on the allotment of shares or placement fees for arranging a loan between a borrower and an investor are examples of such significant acts. Revenue should be recognised when the act has been performed, for example, when the shares have been allotted or the loan arranged. However, fees earned for the completion of a significant act must be distinguished from fees that relate to future performance or to any risk retained. A loan syndication fee, for example, may be earned when the transaction takes place, if the entity that arranges the loan either has no further involvement or retains part of the loan package at the same effective yield for comparable risk as the other participants. If the entity has a lower effective yield for comparable risk than other participants, then some of the syndication fee should be deferred and recognised as revenue as an adjustment to the effective yield of the loan. If the effective yield is higher than the other participants, then part of the yield that relates to the syndication fee should be recognised when the syndication is complete. [IAS 18 App A para 14]. The purpose of such adjustments is to ensure that the effective yield of the loan, for comparable risk, is the same for all participants to the syndicate, so that the syndication fee earned relates only to setting up the syndicate.

11.55 The treatment of accrued interest when an interest bearing security is purchased is discussed in paragraph 5.32.

The substance of transactions with the legal form of a lease

11.56 As discussed in paragraph 7.14 onwards, where two or more transactions are linked they should be treated as a single transaction where that is necessary to understand the transaction's commercial effect. A specific application of this principle is dealt with in SIC 27, 'Evaluating the substance of transactions involving the legal form of a lease'. This SIC was produced in February 2000 to give guidance on a particular type of transaction and became effective on 31 December 2001.

11.57 SIC 27 deals with transactions that have the legal form of a lease but which may not have the substance of one, in that the primary purpose may not be to convey the right to use the asset. Instead, the transaction or series of transactions may, for instance, be intended to secure a tax benefit for the other party (the investor). One example of such a transaction given in SIC 27 is where an entity leases an asset to the investor and leases it back on the same terms and conditions. The entity and the investor have a legally enforceable right to set off amounts owing to each other and an intention to settle the amounts on a net basis. A more complicated arrangement might involve the investor paying a sum equal to the discounted amount of the future rentals up-front and the entity placing the money in an investment account, to which it does not have any further access and from which its own obligation to pay lease rentals is met.

11.58 SIC 27 sets out criteria for determining whether a particular arrangement involves the conveyance of the right to use an asset (when it should be accounted for under IAS 17) or whether it does not, in which case SIC 27 applies. Where the transaction does not convey the right to use an asset, SIC 27 also sets out factors to be considered in determining how any fee receivable by the entity should be recognised. The criteria in paragraph 20 of IAS 18 (see para 5.3 above) should be applied to the facts and circumstances of each arrangement to determine when to recognise a fee as revenue. Factors such as whether there is continuing involvement in the form of significant future performance obligations necessary to earn the fee, whether there are retained risks, the terms of any guarantees given, and the risk having to repay the fee, should be considered.

11.59 Any one of the following factors will indicate that recognising the entire fee as income when received (if received at the beginning of the arrangement) is not appropriate:

■ Obligations of the entity either to perform or to refrain from certain significant activities are conditions of earning the fee received and, therefore, entering into a legally binding arrangement is not the most significant act required by the arrangement.

■ Limitations are put on the use of the underlying asset that have the practical effect of restricting and significantly changing the entity's ability to use the asset.

■ The possibility of having to repay any part of the fee and possibly paying some additional amount is not remote. This may occur, for example, when:

■ the underlying asset is not a specialised asset that has to be used by the entity in its business and, therefore, there is a possibility that the entity may pay an amount to terminate the arrangement early; or

■ the entity is required under the terms of the arrangement, or has discretion, to invest a prepaid amount in assets that carry more than an insignificant amount of risk (for example, currency, interest rate or credit risk). In these circumstances, the risk that the value of the investment at maturity will be insufficient to satisfy the lease payment obligations is not remote and, therefore, there is a possibility that the entity may be required to pay some amount, for example, under a guarantee.

[SIC 27 para 8].

11.60 Where, however, none of the above factors are present and the transaction's substance is that the entity has only a remote risk of having to repay the fee it should reflect the fee as revenue when the conditions for rendering of services in paragraph 20 of IAS 18 are satisfied (see para 5.3). SIC 27 notes that the risk is remote when, for example, the terms of the arrangement require that an amount prepaid by the other party to the arrangement be invested in risk-free assets that are expected to generate sufficient cash flows to satisfy the entity's lease payment obligations. [SIC 27 para 6(b)].

11.61 SIC 27 requires that the fee should be presented in the profit and loss account based on its economic substance and nature. A possible presentation, where the fee is in respect of a transaction that is not in substance a lease, would be to show the fee as other operating income or as finance income. The SIC requires several disclosures to be made in respect of the transactions and assets involved in such a scheme. In respect of fees received it also requires disclosure of the accounting treatment applied to any fee received, the amount recognised in the period and the line item of the profit and loss account in which it is included. [SIC 27 para 10].

11.62 The above discussion of SIC 27 relates mainly to the aspect of the SIC that concerns revenue recognition and does not deal with the consideration in the SIC of whether and when amounts payable and receivable under such arrangements should be netted in the balance sheet.

11.63 An example of disclosure of a scheme accounted for under SIC 27 is Table 7.

Table 7 – Swisscom AG – Annual Report – 31 December 2002

27 Debt (extract)

In 1999, 2000 and 2002, Swisscom entered into cross-border tax lease arrangements with foreign investors relating to some of its fixed and mobile networks. Under the terms of the agreements, which range from 13 to 30 years, Swisscom received a total of USD 3,796 million (CHF 5,249 million) and placed USD 3,536 million (CHF 4,890 million) on deposit. In accordance with Interpretation 27, "Evaluating the substance of transactions involving the legal form of a lease", Swisscom concluded that USD 2,738 million (CHF 3,786 million),which was either irrevocably placed with highly rated securities in trusts or non-refundable payment undertaking agreements with financial institutions with minimal credit risk were signed, lacked economic substance and should not be recognized, as the definition of an asset and liability had not been met. Accordingly, both these assets and liabilities have been removed from the financial statements. Swisscom is not responsible for any performance under these arrangements, other than that which would be done in the normal course

---

of business, and accordingly, recognized the fee as income in the period the transaction was closed. In 2002, Swisscom recorded a fee of CHF 28 million under financial income. At December 31, 2002, debt of CHF 1,463 million and financial assets of CHF 1,104 million were recorded in Swisscom's balance sheet.

Future minimum payments resulting from cross-border tax lease arrangements are due as follows:

CHF in millions	2001	2002
Within one year	90	78
Within 1–2 years	93	84
Within 2–3 years	98	99
Within 3–4 years	101	86
Within 4–5 years	98	90
After 5 years	5 168	4 328
Total future payment commitments	5 648	4 765
Less future interest charges	(4 048)	(3 312)
Total liability from cross-border tax lease arrangements (net present value)	1 600	1 453
Fair value adjustments	-	10
Long-term liability from cross-border tax lease arrangements	1 600	1 463

The weighted average effective interest rates at the balance sheet date were as follows: CHF in millions	2001	2002
Short-term loans	5.85%	5.62%
Swiss Post debt	3.89%	3.65%
Employee savings deposits	2.54%	2.45%
Short-term loans payable to affiliated companies	2.00%	4.64%
Financial liabilities from cross-border tax lease arrangements	6.99%	6.78%

Dividends

11.64 Dividend income should be recognised when the shareholder's right to receive payment is established. [IAS 18 para 30]. In the UK final dividends are usually recommended by the directors and then declared by the shareholders by ordinary resolution. The shareholders cannot declare a dividend that exceeds the amount recommended by the directors. Directors are normally permitted by the entity's articles of association to pay interim dividends without shareholder approval. Normally, therefore, the shareholders' right to a final dividend will be established when it is declared by the shareholders and the right to an interim dividend will be established when it is declared by the directors. If the right to the dividend cannot be established until the income is received, then recognition should be delayed until then.

Example

During the year ended 31 December 20X1 entity A made the following investments in entity B (a listed entity):

1 January	2,000 shares, registered on 28 February 20X1
15 June	5,000 shares, registered on 10 July 20X1
5 October	3,000 shares, registered on 20 December 20X1
29 December	1,000 shares, registration outstanding

The directors of entity B declared an interim dividend on 31 July 20X1 of 0.05 per share, with a last registration date of 30 June 20X1. This dividend declaration does not require shareholder approval. The dividend was paid on 30 September 20X1.

At 31 December 20X1 the directors of entity B proposed a final a dividend of 0.15 per share, with a last registration date of 30 November 20X1. The proposed final dividend was approved by shareholders at the annual general meeting on 31 January 20X2 and the dividend was paid on 31 March 20X2.

Entity A and entity B both have a December year end. What should entity A recognise as dividend income in the year ended 31 December 20X1?

Entity A should recognise dividend income at 31 December 20X1 in respect of the interim dividend, but it should not recognise dividend income in respect of the final dividend.

The entity B directors' declaration of the interim dividend was sufficient to establish entity A's right to receive the dividend. However, entity A is not entitled to receive the final dividend until the shareholders approve it.

Therefore, entity A should recognise a dividend of 100 (2,000 × 0.05) in respect of the interim dividend on the 2,000 shares purchased in January 20X1.

11.65 The situation for parent companies' investments in subsidiaries is no different from that where the shareholding is held as a trade investment. IAS 10, 'Events after the balance sheet date', states that dividends payable to holders of equity instruments (as defined in IAS 32) that are proposed or declared after the balance sheet date should not be recognised as a liability at the balance sheet date [IAS 10 para 11]. Similarly dividends, including dividends from subsidiaries, should not be recognised as receivable if they have not been declared by the balance sheet date.

11.66 The treatment of dividends paid out of pre-acquisition profits is discussed in paragraph 5.33 above.

Shares for services

11.67 Other revenue recognition issues that create particular and new difficulties have arisen in respect of internet companies where the practice of issuing shares for services or accepting equity stakes in exchange for services has been particularly common. The following example illustrates some of these difficulties.

Example

A company provides corporate finance services (for example, assistance in preparing for eventual flotation) to internet companies and proposes to take equity stakes in the internet companies instead of fees. In relation to revenue recognition, what considerations should be taken into account, given the following facts:

■ In some situations securities received will be listed and in other situations they will be unlisted.

■ Some securities will be marketable, whereas some may not be marketable.

■ The company intends to hold the securities for the medium to long-term.

■ There may be restrictions placed on the company's ability to dispose of the securities for a period of time.

The reason for the proposed arrangements is for the company to share in the success of the internet companies it advises and to assist the internet companies by enabling them to obtain advice without having to part with large sums in cash.

IAS 18 states the conditions that need to be satisfied before revenue for services provided is recognised under IAS. These are:

"When the outcome of a transaction involving the rendering of services can be estimated reliably, revenue associated with the transaction should be recognised by reference to the stage of completion of the transaction at the balance sheet date. The outcome of a transaction can be estimated reliably when all the following conditions are satisfied:(a) the amount of revenue can be measured reliably; (b) it is probable that the economic benefits associated with the transaction will flow to the enterprise; (c) the stage of completion of the transaction at the balance sheet date can be measured reliably; and (d) the costs incurred for the transaction and the costs to complete the transaction can be measured reliably."
[IAS 18 para 20].

Other practical applications

The main issue raised by the question is whether or not the different forms of consideration enable the consideration, that is the amount of revenue, to be measured reliably. For the purpose of this example it is assumed that the other conditions above are satisfied. IAS does not distinguish between realised and unrealised profits for the purpose of determining whether a profit is recognised in the income statement or not. Therefore, considerations relating to the distinction between realised and realised profits are not relevant for IAS purposes.

Listed/marketable securities
Where shares are listed/marketable and there is a sufficiently liquid market the consideration can be reliably measured and the revenue should be recognised.

Non-marketable securities
Whether or not revenue arises on the receipt of non-marketable securities will depend on whether a reliable basis exists or can be determined for valuing the securities. Paragraphs 95 to 102 of IAS 39, 'Financial instruments: Recognition and measurement', give guidance on ways in which such a value might be determined. If such a basis exists then the amount of revenue can be reliably measured and should be recognised in the income statement. IAS 39 para 102 refers to the IASB's Framework as stating that *"In many cases cost or value must be estimated: the use of reasonable estimates is an essential part of the preparation of financial statements and does not undermine their reliability"*.

Under UK law, however, only realised profits may be included in the profit and loss account. Such profits are determined by reference to Tech 7/03 (see para 14.6 below). Accordingly where unrealised profits are included in the profit and loss account under IAS this would require a true and fair override of current UK law and the necessary disclosures would need to be made. [CA 85 Sec 226(5) and 4 Sch 15]. However, UK law may be changed before IAS are required to be adopted in the UK such that a true and fair override would not be necessary. (see para 14.2 below).

Costs

Generally under IAS, as explained above, it will be possible to obtain a reliable measurement of the revenue, which will be credited to the income statement. Costs should be charged in the income statement at the same time as the revenue is recorded, in the normal way.

Revenue grants

11.68 How to recognise government grants is covered by IAS 20, 'Accounting for government grants and disclosure of government assistance'. The 'accruals' concept implies that government grants should be recognised in the profit and loss account to match them with the expenditure towards which they are intended to contribute. The relationship between the grant and the related expenditure is, therefore, of paramount importance in establishing the accounting treatment to be adopted. IAS 20 states that government grants should be recognised as income over the periods necessary to match them with the related costs that they are intended to compensate, on a systematic basis. [IAS 20 para 12]. It continues by saying that in most situations the periods over which an entity recognises the costs or expenses related to a government grant are readily ascertainable and thus grants in recognition of specific expenses are recognised as income in the same period as the relevant expense. [IAS 20 para 17].

11.69 Government grants should not be recognised until there is reasonable assurance that the entity will comply with the conditions for their receipt and that the grant will be received. [IAS 20 para 7]. In the event that a grant that has been recognised appears likely to have to be repaid, provision should be made for the estimated liability.

11.70 Difficulties of matching may arise where the grant's terms do not specify precisely the expenditure towards which it is intended to contribute. For example, grants may be awarded to defray project costs comprising both revenue and capital expenditure. Project grants are normally awarded on this basis and may be related to the project's capital expenditure costs and the number of jobs created or safeguarded. In such circumstances, the expenditure eligible for grant aid may be all the costs incurred that are directly attributable to the project. The terms of the grant itself often need to be carefully examined to establish whether the intent is to defray costs or to establish a condition relating to the entire amount of the grant.

Example

A company obtains a grant from an Industrial Development agency for an investment project in Scotland. The project is a building to house a manufacturing plant. The principal terms are that the grant payments relate to the level of capital expenditure and the intention of the grant is to help ensure that imports of the product can be replaced with UK sourced products and to safeguard 500 jobs. The grant will have to be repaid if there is an underspend on capital or if the jobs are not safeguarded until 18 months after the date of the last fixed asset purchase.

This grant is related to capital expenditure. The employment condition should be seen as an additional condition to prevent replacement of labour by capital, rather than as the reason for the grant. If the grant were revenue it would be related to revenue expenditure such as a percentage of the payroll cost or a fixed amount per job safeguarded.

11.71 IAS 20 states that grants are sometimes received as part of a package of financial or fiscal aids where a number of conditions are attached. In such situations, care is needed in identifying the conditions giving rise to costs and expenses that determine the periods over which the grant will be earned. It will sometimes be appropriate to allocate part of the grant on one basis (capital) and part on another (revenue). [IAS 20 para 19]. It will then be possible to account for the grant according to the different types of expenditure towards which it is intended to contribute. If the grant is paid when evidence is produced that certain expenditure has been incurred, then the grant should be matched with that expenditure.

11.72 In certain circumstances the actual expenditure the grant is intended to contribute towards may differ from the expenditure that forms the basis of its payment. For example, the grant may relate to a total project expenditure that may include, in addition to capital expenditure, working capital costs, training costs and removal costs. However, the grant may become payable in instalments on incurring specific amounts of capital expenditure as the project progresses. In this situation, it would be wrong to match the grant with the capital expenditure alone. The most appropriate treatment, therefore, would be to match the grant received rateably with the expenditure towards which the grant is assisting, that is, the grant would have to be spread rateably over the constituent parts of the project expenditure. This treatment accords with IAS 20, which provides, as noted above, that it will sometimes be appropriate to allocate part of a grant on one basis and part on another basis. Therefore, where such evidence exists and is sufficiently persuasive, it is appropriate to match grants received with identified expenditure and this approach should always be preferred.

11.73 Sometimes grants may be payable on a different basis, for example, on the achievement of a non-financial objective. In such situations, the grant should be matched with the identifiable costs of achieving that objective. Such costs must be identified or estimated on a reasonable basis. For example, if a grant is given on condition that jobs are created and maintained for a minimum period, the grant should be matched with the cost of providing the jobs for that period. As a result, a greater proportion of the grant may fall to be recognised in the early stages of the project because of higher non-productive and set-up costs.

11.74 In certain circumstances, government grants may be awarded unconditionally without regard to the entity's future actions, or requirement to incur further costs. Such grants may be given for the immediate financial support, or assistance of an entity, or for the reimbursement of costs previously incurred. They may also be given to finance the general activities of an entity over a specified period, or to compensate for a loss of income. In some instances, the extent of these grants may constitute a major source of revenue for the entity. Where grants are awarded on such a basis, they should be recognised in the profit and loss account of the period in which they become receivable. [IAS 20 para 20].

Emission rights

11.75 In May 2003, the IASB's International Financial Reporting Interpretations Committee (IFRIC) published a draft Interpretation dealing with accounting for emission rights. Emission rights are rights to emit pollutant at a specified level and are allocated by Government to participants in a scheme. Depending on the nature of the scheme, the rights (allowances) are allocated free of charge or participants may pay Government for them. Participants may also buy and sell allowances.

11.76 The proposals in the draft Interpretation are that:

■ Allowances, whether allocated by Government or purchased, are intangible assets that should be accounted for under IAS 38, 'Intangible assets'. Allowances that are allocated at less than fair value should be measured initially at fair value.

■ Where allowances are allocated at less than fair value the difference between the amount paid and the fair value should be treated as a government grant and accounted for under IAS 20, 'Accounting for government grants and disclosure of government assistance'. Therefore, the grant is initially recognised as deferred income in the balance sheet and subsequently taken to income on a systematic basis over the compliance period for which the allowances were allocated. (The draft Interpretation would not permit the grant to be netted against the intangible asset.)

■ A liability should be established for the obligation to deliver allowances equal to emissions that have been made. The liability is accounted for under IAS 37 'Provisions, contingent liabilities and contingent assets'.

Example

Note: this example assumes that the entity uses the allowed alternative treatment in IAS 38 to measure the intangible asset at fair value after its initial recognition.

Entity A is allocated on 1 January 20X0, free of charge, allowances to emit 10,000 tonnes of carbon dioxide during the calendar year 20X0, which is also its financial accounting period. The market price of allowances at 1 January 20X0 is £10 per tonne, giving a fair value of £100,000.

At the half year, 30 June 20X0, the entity has emitted 6,000 tonnes of carbon dioxide and expects its emissions for the full year to be 11,000 tonnes. The market price for allowances has risen to £11 per tonne.

At the year end the entity has emitted 12,000 tonnes and the market price of allowances is £12 per tonne. How should entity A account for the scheme?

Entity A should record the initial receipt of allowances at fair value of £100,000, setting up an intangible asset for this amount and recording a government grant as deferred income for the same amount.

At the half year stage the entity should record a provision for the emissions to date of £66,000 (6000 tonnes at £11 per tonne). The asset of £100,000 is revalued to £110,000 (10,000 tonnes at £11 per tonne). The deferred income is released in the proportion that emissions to date bear to total emissions expected for the year, that is £100,000 times 6,000 divided by 11,000 = £54,545.

At the half year the income statement, therefore, reflects deferred income released of £54,545 less the provision of £66,000, giving a net effect on the income statement for the period of minus £11,455. The revaluation surplus of £10,000 on the intangible asset is taken to equity.

At the full year (and ignoring the half year entries) the entity records a provision for emissions of £144,000 (12,000 tonnes at £12 per tonne). The asset is revalued to £120,000 (10,000 tonnes at £12 per tonne). All of the deferred income of £100,000 is released.

The effect on the income statement for the full year is to record a provision of £144,000 and to release deferred income of £100,000. The revaluation surplus of £20,000 is taken to equity. There is a net effect on the income statement of minus £44,000. Taken together with the revaluation surplus in equity of £20,000 the net figure of £24,000 represents the cost to the entity of excess emissions of 2,000 tonnes times the market price at the year end of £12 per tonne.

If the benchmark treatment in IAS 38 had been used for the intangible asset and, accordingly, it had been measured after its initial recognition at cost less amortisation and/or impairment (cost being fair value on initial recognition for this purpose) there would be no revaluation surplus of £20,000 at the year end and the intangible asset would be stated at £100,000. Because the provision of £144,000 would be settled by using allowances stated at £100,000 (but worth £120,000), the entity would need to pay only £24,000. There would remain a balance of the provision of £20,000 that would be released to the income statement. Thus the net charge in the income statement would be £24,000. Again this represents the cost of the excess emissions of 2000 tonnes times £12 per tonne. The net effect on the performance statements would, therefore, be the same (minus £24,000) whether the benchmark or the alternative accounting treatments in IAS 38 is adopted.

Insurance recoveries

11.77 Amounts receivable from insurance recoveries may represent a significant source of income to a company, especially when disaster strikes. For example, in the event of a factory being destroyed by fire, a company may be insured for the replacement cost of the fixed assets and inventory, which may be higher than the carrying value of the assets, as well as for any consequential loss of profits. Compensation received for loss of profits should be credited in arriving at the operating profit for the period to which it relates and be shown separately (as an exceptional item) if material in accordance with paragraph 16 of IAS 8, 'Net profit or loss for the period, fundamental errors and changes in accounting policies'.

11.78 Insurance proceeds relating to fixed assets should also be credited to the profit and loss account. SIC 14, 'Property, plant and equipment –

Compensation for the impairment or loss of items', states that impairments of property, plant and equipment, related claims for compensation from third parties and any subsequent purchase or construction of replacement assets are separate economic events and should be accounted for as such. Therefore, the impairment of a fixed asset and the insurance proceeds should be disclosed separately in the profit and loss account. In order to comply with IAS 8, the amounts relating to the fixed assets would be shown separately as exceptional items in arriving at operating profit. The gain or loss relating to the inventory destroyed would also be included in operating profit, disclosed separately as an exceptional item, if material.

11.79 When the destroyed assets are replaced, they should be included at their actual replacement cost. There is no justification for deferring recognition of the insurance proceeds to reduce the cost of the replacement assets.

Gifts and capital contributions

11.80 IAS 18 and the Framework exclude changes in equity that relate to contributions from or distributions to owners from the definition of gains and these capital items should, therefore, be excluded from the income statement.

11.81 Contributions from owners are usually in the form of cash, but may also occur when other forms of property are transferred into the business or when equity is accepted in satisfaction of a liability. Such gifts of a capital amount are often made by parent companies to their subsidiaries. What constitutes a capital contribution might be difficult to determine in practice. A genuine gift without condition from a third party unconnected with the receiving company and, therefore, not in the capacity of an owner, should generally be treated as a gift and reported as a profit in the year of receipt. In addition, a receipt by a company might not be a capital contribution where it is repaid shortly thereafter other than by way of distribution and this was envisaged at the time the contribution was made. (But it should be remembered that contributions in kind, rather than in cash, do not give rise to a distributable profit). Such a payment would be a loan, if in effect there is an obligation to transfer economic benefits as the contribution is made on the basis that it will be repaid. On the other hand, a contribution that is made without conditions, but is subsequently repaid by a distribution at the discretion of the receiving company, would be a capital contribution rather than a loan.

11.82 Under IAS 1, 'Presentation of financial statements', capital contributions should be reported in a separate statement showing changes in equity or in the notes. The standard makes it clear that such contributions are not gains of an entity and, therefore, should not be reported in the profit and loss account. It states *Except for changes resulting from transactions with shareholders, such as capital contributions and dividends, the overall change in equity represents the total gains and losses generated by the enterprise's activities during the period.* [IAS 1 para 87].

11.83 Nevertheless, it appears that where the amount is received in cash it is legally a realised profit and as such can be taken into account in determining whether a company has sufficient distributable reserves to pay a dividend. Where, however, a contribution is in the form of an asset (for example, shares in a subsidiary) that is not either cash or readily convertible into cash, the contribution is not a realised profit and may not, therefore, be taken into account in determining distributable profits. It is best recorded in a separate reserve to distinguish it from other reserves, because of its difference in nature.

11.84 It seems logical that in the paying company (in a group of companies) the opposite accounting treatment should be adopted. Therefore, the contribution should not be recorded as an expense in the profit and loss account, but should be added to the cost of the investment in the subsidiary. Only if there is an impairment in the underlying value of the investment in the subsidiary would the investing company need to make a provision against its carrying value.

11.85 Gifts in the form of grants may also be given to a company to help finance a particular asset or specific profit and loss account expenditure.

When these grants are given by government, including inter-governmental agencies and EU bodies, guidance on the accounting treatment is contained in IAS 20, which differentiates between the treatment for revenue and capital based grants. The treatment of revenue grants is discussed from paragraph 11.68. Payments given to companies from sources other than government should be subject to similar analysis since IAS 20 is indicative of best practice for accounting for grants and assistance from other sources. Thus, for example, a non-refundable payment by a third party franchisor to assist the franchisee with the purchase of specific assets would be more in the nature of a grant than a capital contribution.

Chapter 12

Disclosure

12.1   IAS 18 requires disclosure of the accounting policies adopted for the recognition of revenue, which should include a description of the methods used to determine the stage of completion of transactions that involve the rendering of services. [IAS 18 para 35(a)].

12.2   The standard also requires disclosure of each significant category of revenue that has been recognised in the period, including revenue from:

- Sale of goods.

- Rendering of services.

- Interest.

- Royalties.

- Dividends.

The amount of revenue derived from exchanges of goods or services, which is included in each of the significant categories of revenue, should also be disclosed.

[IAS 18 paras 35(b),(c)].

12.3   Revenue grants (see para 11.68 above) should be presented in the profit and loss account either separately or under a general heading such as 'Other income'. Alternatively, they may be deducted in reporting the related expense. [IAS 20 para 29].

12.4 Examples of disclosure of accounting policies are given in Tables 8 and 9.

Table 8 – Bayer AG – Annual Report – 31 December 2002

NOTES TO THE STATEMENTS OF INCOME (extract)

[1] Net sales

Sales are recognized upon delivery of goods or rendering of services to third parties and are reported net of sales taxes and rebates. Revenues from contracts that contain customer acceptance provisions are deferred until customer acceptance occurs or the contractual acceptance period has lapsed. Allocations to provisions for rebates to customers are recognized in the period in which the related sales are recorded based on the contract terms. Payments relating to the sale or out licensing of technologies or technological expertise – once the respective agreements have become effective – are immediately recognized in income if all rights to the technologies and all obligations resulting from them have been relinquished under the contract terms. However, if rights to the technologies continue to exist or obligations resulting from them have yet to be fulfilled, the payments received are recorded in line with the actual circumstances.

Table 9 – Roche Holding Ltd – Annual Report – 31 December 2002

Revenues and cost of sales

Sales represent amounts received and receivable for goods supplied and services rendered to customers after deducting trade discounts and volume rebates and excluding sales and value added taxes. Cash discounts are recorded as marketing and distribution expenses. Revenues from the sale of products are recognised upon transfer to the customer of significant risks and rewards, usually upon shipment. Royalty income is recognised on an accrual basis in accordance with the economic substance of the agreement. Other revenues are recorded as earned or as the services are performed. Cost of sales includes the corresponding direct production costs and related production overhead of goods manufactured and services rendered.

In-licensing, milestone and other up-front receipts and payments

Certain Group companies, notably Genentech, receive from third-parties up-front, milestone and other similar non-refundable payments relating to the sale or licensing of products or technology. Revenue associated with performance milestones is recognised based on achievement of the milestones, as defined in the respective agreements. Revenue from non-refundable up-front payments and licence fees is initially reported as deferred income and is recognised in income as earned over the period of the development collaboration or the manufacturing obligation. Payments made by Group companies to third parties and associated companies for such items are charged against income as research and development costs unless it is probable that future economic benefits will flow to the Group, which is normally evidenced by regulatory approval. In this case they are capitalised as development costs and amortised as described above. In practice this means that most in-licensing and milestone payments for pharmaceutical products are expensed as incurred, as in most cases they have not yet gained regulatory approval. Receipts and payments between consolidated subsidiaries, such as between Genentech and other Roche Group subsidiaries, are eliminated on consolidation.

12.5 IAS 1, 'Presentation of financial statements', requires the profit and loss account of a company or a group to include specified items. IAS 8, 'Net profit or loss for the period, fundamental errors and changes in accounting policies', also affects the disclosure requirements of the profit and loss account.

12.6 In most situations, 'Revenue' in the profit and loss account will include revenue from sale of goods and provision of services, and interest will be included under a heading 'finance costs'. However, the classification adopted will depend on the nature of a company's business and, for example, interest income would generally form part of a bank's 'revenue'.

12.7 IAS 18 states that revenue reflects only the gross inflows of economic benefits received or receivable by an entity on its own account. It, therefore, excludes amounts collected on behalf of third parties such as sales taxes, goods and services taxes and value added taxes. [IAS 18 para

8]. If a company intends to show also its revenue, grossed up for the VAT element as additional information, it should, therefore, show the VAT relevant to that revenue as a deduction in arriving at the revenue exclusive of VAT. Although this treatment is not common, it is practised by companies that may wish to emphasise the amount of VAT and duty that is included in their 'gross' revenue.

12.8   Where a company acts as an agent or broker, such as a travel agent or stock broker, it should not include the gross value of the contracts in its revenue, but only the commission or margin that it charges on each deal. The inclusion of such amounts in revenue is consistent with IAS 18, which excludes amounts collected on behalf of third parties from its definition of revenue. An estate agent, for example, should only recognise the commission that is earned on properties sold.

12.9   The issue of agency versus principal is particularly pronounced in e-businesses. Further discussion regarding criteria that may be relevant to determining whether companies are acting as agents or principals and, accordingly, whether they should report revenue net or gross is contained in paragraph 10.1 onwards.

Chapter 13

First-time adoption of IFRS

13.1   In the UK all listed companies are required to apply EU-adopted international financial reporting standards in their consolidated financial statements for accounting periods beginning on or after 1 January 2005.

13.2   IFRS 1, 'First-time adoption of international financial reporting standards', does not contain any specific exemptions in respect of IAS 18. In practice, UK companies will normally have adopted policies that are consistent with IAS 18, because that standard is looked to for guidance, in the absence of a specific UK standard. Therefore, UK companies are unlikely to have many issues arising as a result of adopting IAS 18.

Chapter 14

Companies Act 1985 requirements

14.1 The Companies Act 1985 is more restrictive than IAS 18 in terms of profits that may be included in the profit and loss account. Schedule 4 paragraph 12(a) states: *". . .only profits realised at the balance sheet date shall be included in the profit and loss account"*. IAS 18 contains no such restriction and, therefore, there could be instances where revenue that represents an unrealised profit might be included in the profit and loss account under IFRS, which the provisions of the Act would not permit to be included.

14.2 However, it is likely that UK law will change so as to permit companies that are required to adopt IFRS to substitute the requirements and rules in IFRS for most of the Companies Act 1985 Schedule 4 requirements. Furthermore, if other companies are permitted to voluntarily adopt IFRS then in practice, it is likely that UK law will be amended to remove this restriction. If not, then a true and fair override of the Act's requirements would be necessary for these companies in order to comply with IFRS, when an unrealised profit is included in the profit and loss account.

14.3 Whether this difference between the Act's requirements and IAS 18 has any effect in practice is debatable and examples of the effect are not immediately apparent. This is because IAS 18 itself requires that for revenue to be recognised it should be capable of reliable measurement and it should be probable that the economic benefits associated with the transaction will flow to the entity. It is more likely that the difference will be more important in the context of accounting for revaluation gains such as those on investment property that are covered by IAS 40.

14.4 However, there is a further effect of the difference that is likely to have a continuing impact if companies are required or permitted to prepare their individual financial statements under IFRS. UK rules on distributions require generally that distributions may only be made out of realised profits. The Act states that for the purpose of determining realised profits reference should be made to:

"...principles generally accepted, at the time when the accounts are prepared, with respect to the determination for accounting purposes of realised profits or losses." [Sec 262(3)].

The effect of the above Schedule 4 requirement has been that generally the profit and loss account is made up of realised and, therefore, distributable profits. If the profit and loss account in future includes unrealised profits it will be necessary to keep track of such profits and exclude them when considering profits available for distribution.

14.5 The term 'principles generally accepted' is not elaborated on further in the Act. However, it has been given a judicial interpretation, as being *"...principles which are generally regarded as permissible or legitimate by the accountancy profession. That is sufficient even though only one company actually applies it in practice".* [Lord Denning, MR, in Associated Portland Cement Manufacturers Ltd v Price Commission. [1975] ICR 27]. Thus an accounting treatment does not necessarily have to be very common as long as it is thought to be acceptable by accountants. In March 2003, the ICAEW and ICAS issued guidance in Tech 7/03, 'Guidance on the determination of realised profits and losses in the context of distributions under the Companies Act 1985'.

14.6 Tech 7/03 states that a profit is realised where it arises from:

- A transaction where the consideration received by a company is 'qualifying consideration'. Qualifying consideration is defined as:

    - Cash.

    - An asset for which there is a liquid market (as defined below).

- The release, or the settlement or assumption by another party, of all or part of a liability of the company, unless:

  - the liability arose from the purchase of an asset that does not meet the definition of qualifying consideration and has not been disposed of for qualifying consideration; and

  - the purchase and release are part of a group or series of transactions or arrangements. A realised profit will arise only where the overall commercial effect on the company satisfies the definition of realised profit set out in the guidance.

  - An amount receivable in any of the above forms of consideration where the debtor is capable of settling the receivable within a reasonable period of time, there is a reasonable certainty that the debtor will be capable of settling when called upon to do so and there is an expectation that the receivable will be settled.

- An event that results in a company receiving qualifying consideration in circumstances where no consideration is given by the company (for example, a 'capital contribution').

- The recognition in the profit and loss account of the profit arising from the use of the marking to market method of accounting, in those cases where the method is properly adopted in accordance with law and generally accepted accounting principles.

- The translation of a monetary asset that comprises qualifying consideration or a liability denominated in a foreign currency.

- The reversal of a loss previously regarded as realised (for example, writing back a charge for impairment or for the release of a provision for a specific loss).

Companies Act 1985 requirements

- A profit previously regarded as unrealised and which has not been capitalised (for example, a revaluation reserve, merger reserve or other similar reserve) becoming realised as a result of:

  - Consideration previously received by the company becoming qualifying consideration.

  - The related asset being disposed of in a transaction where the company receives qualifying consideration.

  - A realised loss being recognised on the scrapping or disposal of the related asset.

  - A realised loss being recognised on the write-down for depreciation, amortisation, diminution in value or impairment of the related asset.

  - The distribution in *specie* of the asset to which the unrealised profit relates.

In such situations, the appropriate proportion of the related unrealised profit becomes a realised profit.

- A reduction or cancellation of capital (for example, share capital, share premium account or capital redemption reserve) that is credited to reserves and the reduction or cancellation is confirmed by the court (except to the extent that, and for as long as, the company has undertaken that it will not treat the reserve arising as a realised profit, or where the court has directed that it shall not be treated as a realised profit).

- A reduction or cancellation of capital (for example, share capital, share premium account or capital redemption reserve) that is undertaken by an unlimited company without confirmation by the court. Any credit to reserves represents a realised profit to the extent that the consideration received for the capital:

■ Was qualifying consideration.

■ Has subsequently become qualifying consideration.

■ Has subsequently been written off (for example, by way of depreciation) and the loss arising has been treated as realised.

■ Was originally paid up either by a capitalisation of realised profits or by a capitalisation of unrealised profits or reserves that, had they not been capitalised, would subsequently have become realised.

14.7 As used above, the expression 'asset for which there is a liquid market' means that:

■ The asset belongs to a homogeneous population of assets that are equivalent in all material respects.

■ An active market, evidenced by frequent transactions, exists for that asset.

■ The market has sufficient depth to absorb the asset without a significant effect on the price that underpins the carrying amount.

■ The company is capable of readily disposing of the asset and it can do so without curtailing or disrupting its business.

■ The asset is readily convertible into known amounts of cash at or close to its carrying amount.

14.8 Tech 7/03 also provides fuller definitions of some of the terms used in the above extract. It is the most comprehensive update on realised profits for many years and also deals with other issues, for example: intra-group transactions; the impact of a change in circumstances on realised profits; the effect on dividends of a new accounting standard;

foreign exchange profits and losses; hedging; and goodwill (and negative goodwill) in a company's individual financial statements.

14.9 IAS 18 does not permit the current UK practice of recognising dividends receivable on equity shares at the time they are proposed. Instead dividends receivable would be recognised when declared. The present UK practice is based on the need to comply with UK law, which requires proposed dividends to be included in the profit and loss account of the paying company (and, therefore, to be shown as a liability). It is, therefore, logical that such dividends are also shown as revenue by the receiving company. It is likely that the UK law will be changed to enable the IFRS treatment (which is to recognise dividends on equity shares when declared) to be adopted in the UK.

14.10 IAS 18 requires disclosure of each significant category of revenue to be disclosed, including revenue from sale of goods, provision of services, interest, royalties and dividends. The Act also has specific disclosure requirements for:

■ Turnover (defined in section 262 of the Act as *"...the amounts derived from the provision of goods and services falling within the company's ordinary activities, after deduction of (i) trade discounts, (ii) value added tax and (iii) any other taxes based on the amounts so derived"*).

■ Other operating income.

■ Interest.

Chapter 15

Comparison of IAS 18 and UK GAAP

15.1   There is, as yet, no UK standard dealing specifically with revenue recognition, although FRS 5, 'Reporting the substance of transactions', deals with some specific types of transaction, including consignment stocks and sale and repurchase agreements. Several UITF Abstracts also deal with, or touch on, issues relating to revenue recognition and the related matter of cost recognition. These include:

■   UITF 24, 'Accounting for start-up costs'.

■   UITF 26, 'Barter transactions for advertising'.

■   UITF 28, 'Operating lease incentives'.

■   UITF 34, 'Pre-contract costs'.

■   UITF 36, 'Contracts for sales of capacity'.

15.2   IAS 18 is generally consistent with the principle set out in the ASB's 'Statement of principles for financial reporting' and, in the absence of a UK standard, is used widely, together with US GAAP, by UK companies for guidance on revenue recognition.

15.3   As noted in paragraph 14.9, IAS 18 would not permit the current UK practice of recognising dividends receivable on equity shares at the time they are proposed. Instead dividends receivable are recognised when declared under IFRS.

15.4   In July 2001 the ASB issued a discussion paper, 'Revenue recognition', that made proposals with the aim of establishing a framework within which to address consistently revenue issues arising in different contexts. It is unlikely, however, that this will proceed to become a UK standard. Instead, the discussion paper will be used to help establish the UK position so that the ASB may work with the IASB in its development of a new international financial reporting standard. The IASB has a current project on revenue recognition which is being carried out jointly with the FASB.

15.5 In the meantime, in February 2003, the ASB issued an exposure draft, 'Amendment to FRS 5, 'Reporting the substance of transactions': Revenue recognition'. This is intended as an interim step to provide guidance in the UK until a new standard is developed internationally. The exposure draft takes the form of a proposed additional application note to FRS 5 (Application note G). It sets out the basic principles of revenue recognition and is intended to codify existing best practice. However, there is a change in emphasis as the guidance is based on an assets and liabilities approach. This means that an entity should measure revenue according to either an increase in assets (such as a debtor) or a decrease in liabilities (for instance, the release of a liability initially set up when a customer pays in advance), which arises from its performance under the contractual arrangements (formal or informal) it has entered into with its customer. The exposure draft also includes specific guidance for five types of transaction that give rise to turnover that have been subject to differing interpretations in practice. These are; long-term contractual performance; separation and linking of contractual arrangements; bill and hold arrangements; sales with right of return; and the presentation of turnover by principals and agents.

Appendix

IAS 18 Revenue

In 1998, IAS 39 *Financial Instruments: Recognition and Measurement* amended paragraph 11 of IAS 18 by inserting a cross-reference to IAS 39.

In May 1999, IAS 10 *Events After the Balance Sheet Date* amended paragraph 36. The amended text is effective for annual financial statements covering periods beginning on or after 1 January 2000.

In January 2001, IAS 41 *Agriculture* amended paragraph 6. IAS 41 is effective for annual financial statements covering periods beginning on or after 1 January 2003.

The following SIC Interpretations relate to IAS 18:

• SIC-27: *Evaluating the Substance of Transactions in the Legal Form of a Lease*

• SIC-31: *Revenue - Barter Transactions Involving Advertising Services*

Contents

International Accounting Standard IAS 18

Revenue

International accounting standard IAS 18

Revenue

> International Accounting Standard 18 *Revenue* (IAS 18) is set out in paragraphs 1-37 and Appendix A. All the paragraphs have equal authority but retain the IASC format of the Standard when it was adopted by the IASB. IAS 18 should be read in the context of its objective, the *Preface to International Financial Reporting Standards* and the *Framework for the Preparation and Presentation of Financial Statements*. These provide a basis for selecting and applying accounting policies in the absence of explicit guidance.

Objective

Income is defined in the *Framework for the Preparation and Presentation of Financial Statements* as increases in economic benefits during the accounting period in the form of inflows or enhancements of assets or decreases of liabilities that result in increases in equity, other than those relating to contributions from equity participants. Income encompasses both revenue and gains. Revenue is income that arises in the course of ordinary activities of an enterprise and is referred to by a variety of different names including sales, fees, interest, dividends and royalties. The objective of this Standard is to prescribe the accounting treatment of revenue arising from certain types of transactions and events.

The primary issue in accounting for revenue is determining when to recognise revenue. Revenue is recognised when it is probable that future economic benefits will flow to the enterprise and these benefits can be measured reliably. This Standard identifies the circumstances in which these criteria will be met and, therefore, revenue will be recognised. It also provides practical guidance on the application of these criteria.

Scope

1. This Standard should be applied in accounting for revenue arising from the following transactions and events:

(a)   *the sale of goods;*

(b)   *the rendering of services; and*

(c)   *the use by others of enterprise assets yielding interest, royalties and dividends.*

2. This Standard supersedes IAS 18 *Revenue Recognition* approved in 1982.

3. Goods includes goods produced by the enterprise for the purpose of sale and goods purchased for resale, such as merchandise purchased by a retailer or land and other property held for resale.

4. The rendering of services typically involves the performance by the enterprise of a contractually agreed task over an agreed period of time.

The services may be rendered within a single period or over more than one period. Some contracts for the rendering of services are directly related to construction contracts, for example, those for the services of project managers and architects. Revenue arising from these contracts is not dealt with in this Standard but is dealt with in accordance with the requirements for construction contracts as specified in IAS 11 *Construction Contracts*.

5. The use by others of enterprise assets gives rise to revenue in the form of:

(a)   interest - charges for the use of cash or cash equivalents or amounts due to the enterprise;

(b)   royalties - charges for the use of long-term assets of the enterprise, for example, patents, trademarks, copyrights and computer software; and

(c)   dividends - distributions of profits to holders of equity investments in proportion to their holdings of a particular class of capital.

6. This Standard does not deal with revenue arising from:

(a)   lease agreements (see IAS 17 *Leases*);

(b)   dividends arising from investments which are accounted for under the equity method (see IAS 28 *Accounting for Investments in Associates*);

(c)   insurance contracts of insurance enterprises;

(d)   changes in the fair value of financial assets and financial liabilities or their disposal (see IAS 39 *Financial Instruments: Recognition and Measurement*);

(e)   changes in the value of other current assets;

(f)   initial recognition and from changes in the fair value of biological assets related to agricultural activity (see IAS 41 *Agriculture*);

(g)   initial recognition of agricultural produce (see IAS 41 *Agriculture*); and

(h)   the extraction of mineral ores.

Definitions

7. The following terms are used in this Standard with the meanings specified:

<u>Revenue</u> is the gross inflow of economic benefits during the period arising in the course of the ordinary activities of an enterprise when those inflows result in increases in equity, other than increases relating to contributions from equity participants.

<u>Fair value</u> is the amount for which an asset could be exchanged, or a liability settled, between knowledgeable, willing parties in an arm's length transaction.

8. Revenue includes only the gross inflows of economic benefits received and receivable by the enterprise on its own account. Amounts collected on behalf of third parties such as sales taxes, goods and services taxes and value added taxes are not economic benefits which flow to the enterprise and do not result in increases in equity. Therefore, they are excluded from revenue. Similarly, in an agency relationship, the gross inflows of economic benefits include amounts collected on behalf of the principal and which do not result in increases in equity for the enterprise. The amounts collected on behalf of the principal are not revenue. Instead, revenue is the amount of commission.

Measurement of Revenue

***9. Revenue should be measured at the fair value of the consideration received or receivable.*[1]**

10. The amount of revenue arising on a transaction is usually determined by agreement between the enterprise and the buyer or user of the asset. It is measured at the fair value of the consideration received or receivable taking into account the amount of any trade discounts and volume rebates allowed by the enterprise.

11. In most cases, the consideration is in the form of cash or cash equivalents and the amount of revenue is the amount of cash or cash equivalents received or receivable. However, when the inflow of cash or cash equivalents is deferred, the fair value of the consideration may be less than the nominal amount of cash received or receivable. For example, an enterprise may provide interest free credit to the buyer or accept a note receivable bearing a below-market interest rate from the buyer as consideration for the sale of goods. When the arrangement effectively constitutes a financing transaction, the fair value of the consideration is determined by discounting all future receipts using an imputed rate of interest. The imputed rate of interest is the more clearly determinable of either:

(a)   the prevailing rate for a similar instrument of an issuer with a similar credit rating; or

(b)   a rate of interest that discounts the nominal amount of the instrument to the current cash sales price of the goods or services.

The difference between the fair value and the nominal amount of the consideration is recognised as interest revenue in accordance with paragraphs 29 and 30 and in accordance with IAS 39 *Financial Instruments: Recognition and Measurement.*

---

1   See also SIC-31 *Revenue – Barter Transactions Involving Advertising Services.*

12. When goods or services are exchanged or swapped for goods or services which are of a similar nature and value, the exchange is not regarded as a transaction which generates revenue. This is often the case with commodities like oil or milk where suppliers exchange or swap inventories in various locations to fulfil demand on a timely basis in a particular location. When goods are sold or services are rendered in exchange for dissimilar goods or services, the exchange is regarded as a transaction which generates revenue. The revenue is measured at the fair value of the goods or services received, adjusted by the amount of any cash or cash equivalents transferred. When the fair value of the goods or services received cannot be measured reliably, the revenue is measured at the fair value of the goods or services given up, adjusted by the amount of any cash or cash equivalents transferred.

Identification of the Transaction

13. The recognition criteria in this Standard are usually applied separately to each transaction. However, in certain circumstances, it is necessary to apply the recognition criteria to the separately identifiable components of a single transaction in order to reflect the substance of the transaction. For example, when the selling price of a product includes an identifiable amount for subsequent servicing, that amount is deferred and recognised as revenue over the period during which the service is performed. Conversely, the recognition criteria are applied to two or more transactions together when they are linked in such a way that the commercial effect cannot be understood without reference to the series of transactions as a whole. For example, an enterprise may sell goods and, at the same time, enter into a separate agreement to repurchase the goods at a later date, thus negating the substantive effect of the transaction; in such a case, the two transactions are dealt with together.

Sale of Goods

14. Revenue from the sale of goods should be recognised when all the following conditions have been satisfied:

(a)   *the enterprise has transferred to the buyer the significant risks and rewards of ownership of the goods;*

(b)   *the enterprise retains neither continuing managerial involvement to the degree usually associated with ownership nor effective control over the goods sold;*

(c)   *the amount of revenue can be measured reliably;*

(d)   *it is probable that the economic benefits associated with the transaction will flow to the enterprise; and*

(e)   *the costs incurred or to be incurred in respect of the transaction can be measured reliably.*

15. The assessment of when an enterprise has transferred the significant risks and rewards of ownership to the buyer requires an examination of the circumstances of the transaction. In most cases, the transfer of the risks and rewards of ownership coincides with the transfer of the legal title or the passing of possession to the buyer. This is the case for most retail sales. In other cases, the transfer of risks and rewards of ownership occurs at a different time from the transfer of legal title or the passing of possession.

16. If the enterprise retains significant risks of ownership, the transaction is not a sale and revenue is not recognised. An enterprise may retain a significant risk of ownership in a number of ways. Examples of situations in which the enterprise may retain the significant risks and rewards of ownership are:

(a)   when the enterprise retains an obligation for unsatisfactory performance not covered by normal warranty provisions;

(b)   when the receipt of the revenue from a particular sale is contingent on the derivation of revenue by the buyer from its sale of the goods;

(c)   when the goods are shipped subject to installation and the installation is a significant part of the contract which has not yet been completed by the enterprise; and

(d)   when the buyer has the right to rescind the purchase for a reason specified in the sales contract and the enterprise is uncertain about the probability of return.

17. If an enterprise retains only an insignificant risk of ownership, the transaction is a sale and revenue is recognised. For example, a seller may retain the legal title to the goods solely to protect the collectability of the amount due. In such a case, if the enterprise has transferred the significant risks and rewards of ownership, the transaction is a sale and revenue is recognised. Another example of an enterprise retaining only an insignificant risk of ownership may be a retail sale when a refund is offered if the customer is not satisfied. Revenue in such cases is recognised at the time of sale provided the seller can reliably estimate future returns and recognises a liability for returns based on previous experience and other relevant factors.

18. Revenue is recognised only when it is probable that the economic benefits associated with the transaction will flow to the enterprise. In some cases, this may not be probable until the consideration is received or until an uncertainty is removed. For example, it may be uncertain that a foreign governmental authority will grant permission to remit the consideration from a sale in a foreign country. When the permission is granted, the uncertainty is removed and revenue is recognised. However, when an uncertainty arises about the collectability of an amount already included in revenue, the uncollectable amount or the amount in respect of which recovery has ceased to be probable is recognised as an expense, rather than as an adjustment of the amount of revenue originally recognised.

19. Revenue and expenses that relate to the same transaction or other event are recognised simultaneously; this process is commonly referred to as the matching of revenues and expenses. Expenses, including warranties and other costs to be incurred after the shipment of the goods

can normally be measured reliably when the other conditions for the recognition of revenue have been satisfied. However, revenue cannot be recognised when the expenses cannot be measured reliably; in such circumstances, any consideration already received for the sale of the goods is recognised as a liability.

Rendering of Services

20. When the outcome of a transaction involving the rendering of services can be estimated reliably, revenue associated with the transaction should be recognised by reference to the stage of completion of the transaction at the balance sheet date. The outcome of a transaction can be estimated reliably when all the following conditions are satisfied:

(a)   the amount of revenue can be measured reliably;

(b)   it is probable that the economic benefits associated with the transaction will flow to the enterprise;

(c)   the stage of completion of the transaction at the balance sheet date can be measured reliably; and

(d)   the costs incurred for the transaction and the costs to complete the transaction can be measured reliably. [2], [3]

21. The recognition of revenue by reference to the stage of completion of a transaction is often referred to as the percentage of completion method. Under this method, revenue is recognised in the accounting periods in which the services are rendered. The recognition of revenue on this basis provides useful information on the extent of service activity and performance during a period. IAS 11 *Construction Contracts* also requires the recognition of revenue on this basis. The requirements of that

---

2   See also SIC-27 *Evaluating the Substance of Transactions in the Legal Form of a Lease.*
3   See also SIC-31 *Revenue – Barber Transactions Involving Advertising Services.*

Standard are generally applicable to the recognition of revenue and the associated expenses for a transaction involving the rendering of services.

22. Revenue is recognised only when it is probable that the economic benefits associated with the transaction will flow to the enterprise. However, when an uncertainty arises about the collectability of an amount already included in revenue, the uncollectable amount, or the amount in respect of which recovery has ceased to be probable, is recognised as an expense, rather than as an adjustment of the amount of revenue originally recognised.

23. An enterprise is generally able to make reliable estimates after it has agreed to the following with the other parties to the transaction:

(a)   each party's enforceable rights regarding the service to be provided and received by the parties;

(b)   the consideration to be exchanged; and

(c)   the manner and terms of settlement.

It is also usually necessary for the enterprise to have an effective internal financial budgeting and reporting system. The enterprise reviews and, when necessary, revises the estimates of revenue as the service is performed. The need for such revisions does not necessarily indicate that the outcome of the transaction cannot be estimated reliably.

24. The stage of completion of a transaction may be determined by a variety of methods. An enterprise uses the method that measures reliably the services performed. Depending on the nature of the transaction, the methods may include:

(a)   surveys of work performed;

(b)   services performed to date as a percentage of total services to be performed; or

(c)   the proportion that costs incurred to date bear to the estimated total costs of the transaction. Only costs that reflect services performed to date are included in costs incurred to date. Only costs that reflect services performed or to be performed are included in the estimated total costs of the transaction.

Progress payments and advances received from customers often do not reflect the services performed.

25. For practical purposes, when services are performed by an indeterminate number of acts over a specified period of time, revenue is recognised on a straight line basis over the specified period unless there is evidence that some other method better represents the stage of completion. When a specific act is much more significant than any other acts, the recognition of revenue is postponed until the significant act is executed.

26. When the outcome of the transaction involving the rendering of services cannot be estimated reliably, revenue should be recognised only to the extent of the expenses recognised that are recoverable.

27. During the early stages of a transaction, it is often the case that the outcome of the transaction cannot be estimated reliably. Nevertheless, it may be probable that the enterprise will recover the transaction costs incurred. Therefore, revenue is recognised only to the extent of costs incurred that are expected to be recoverable. As the outcome of the transaction cannot be estimated reliably, no profit is recognised.

28. When the outcome of a transaction cannot be estimated reliably and it is not probable that the costs incurred will be recovered, revenue is not recognised and the costs incurred are recognised as an expense. When the uncertainties that prevented the outcome of the contract being estimated reliably no longer exist, revenue is recognised in accordance with paragraph 20 rather than in accordance with paragraph 26.

Interest, Royalties and Dividends

29. Revenue arising from the use by others of enterprise assets yielding interest, royalties and dividends should be recognised on the bases set out in paragraph 30 when:

(a)   it is probable that the economic benefits associated with the transaction will flow to the enterprise; and

(b)   the amount of the revenue can be measured reliably.

30. Revenue should be recognised on the following bases:

(a)   interest should be recognised on a time proportion basis that takes into account the effective yield on the asset;

(b)   royalties should be recognised on an accrual basis in accordance with the substance of the relevant agreement; and

(c)   dividends should be recognised when the shareholder's right to receive payment is established.

31. The effective yield on an asset is the rate of interest required to discount the stream of future cash receipts expected over the life of the asset to equate to the initial carrying amount of the asset. Interest revenue includes the amount of amortisation of any discount, premium or other difference between the initial carrying amount of a debt security and its amount at maturity.

32. When unpaid interest has accrued before the acquisition of an interest-bearing investment, the subsequent receipt of interest is allocated between pre-acquisition and post-acquisition periods; only the post-acquisition portion is recognised as revenue. When dividends on equity securities are declared from pre-acquisition net income, those dividends are deducted from the cost of the securities. If it is difficult to make such an allocation except on an arbitrary basis, dividends are recognised as

revenue unless they clearly represent a recovery of part of the cost of the equity securities.

33. Royalties accrue in accordance with the terms of the relevant agreement and are usually recognised on that basis unless, having regard to the substance of the agreement, it is more appropriate to recognise revenue on some other systematic and rational basis.

34. Revenue is recognised only when it is probable that the economic benefits associated with the transaction will flow to the enterprise. However, when an uncertainty arises about the collectability of an amount already included in revenue, the uncollectable amount, or the amount in respect of which recovery has ceased to be probable, is recognised as an expense, rather than as an adjustment of the amount of revenue originally recognised.

Disclosure

35. An enterprise should disclose:

(a)   the accounting policies adopted for the recognition of revenue including the methods adopted to determine the stage of completion of transactions involving the rendering of services;

(b)   the amount of each significant category of revenue recognised during the period including revenue arising from:

  (i)   the sale of goods;

  (ii)   the rendering of services;

  (iii)   interest;

  (iv)   royalties;

  (v)   dividends; and

(c)   the amount of revenue arising from exchanges of goods or services included in each significant category of revenue.

36. An enterprise discloses any contingent liabilities and contingent assets in accordance with IAS 37 *Provisions, Contingent Liabilities and Contingent Assets*. Contingent liabilities and contingent assets may arise from items such as warranty costs, claims, penalties or possible losses.

Effective Date

37. This International Accounting Standard becomes operative for financial statements covering periods beginning on or after 1 January 1995.

Appendix A

The appendix is illustrative only and does not form part of the Standard. The purpose of the appendix is to illustrate the application of the Standard to assist in clarifying its meaning in a number of commercial situations. The examples focus on particular aspects of a transaction and are not a comprehensive discussion of all the relevant factors which might influence the recognition of revenue. The examples generally assume that the amount of revenue can be measured reliably, it is probable that the economic benefits will flow to the enterprise and the costs incurred or to be incurred can be measured reliably. The examples do not modify or override the Standard.

Sale of Goods

The law in different countries may mean the recognition criteria in this Standard are met at different times. In particular, the law may determine the point in time at which the enterprise transfers the significant risks and rewards of ownership. Therefore, the examples in this section of the appendix need to be read in the context of the laws relating to the sale of goods in the country in which the transaction takes place.

1. 'Bill and hold' sales, in which delivery is delayed at the buyer's request but the buyer takes title and accepts billing.

Revenue is recognised when the buyer takes title, provided:

(a)   it is probable that delivery will be made;

(b)   the item is on hand, identified and ready for delivery to the buyer at the time the sale is recognised;

(c)   the buyer specifically acknowledges the deferred delivery instructions; and

(d)   the usual payment terms apply.

Revenue is not recognised when there is simply an intention to acquire or manufacture the goods in time for delivery.

2. *Goods shipped subject to conditions.*

(a)   *installation and inspection.*

Revenue is normally recognised when the buyer accepts delivery, and installation and inspection are complete. However, revenue is recognised immediately upon the buyer's acceptance of delivery when:

(i)   the installation process is simple in nature, for example the installation of a factory tested television receiver which only requires unpacking and connection of power and antennae; or

(ii)   the inspection is performed only for purposes of final determination of contract prices, for example, shipments of iron ore, sugar or soya beans.

(b)   *on approval when the buyer has negotiated a limited right of return.*

If there is uncertainty about the possibility of return, revenue is recognised when the shipment has been formally accepted by the buyer or the goods have been delivered and the time period for rejection has elapsed.

(c)   *consignment sales under which the recipient (buyer) undertakes to sell the goods on behalf of the shipper (seller).*

Revenue is recognised by the shipper when the goods are sold by the recipient to a third party.

(d)   *cash on delivery sales.*

Revenue is recognised when delivery is made and cash is received by the seller or its agent.

3. Lay away sales under which the goods are delivered only when the buyer makes the final payment in a series of instalments.

Revenue from such sales is recognised when the goods are delivered. However, when experience indicates that most such sales are consummated, revenue may be recognised when a significant deposit is received provided the goods are on hand, identified and ready for delivery to the buyer.

4. Orders when payment (or partial payment) is received in advance of delivery for goods not presently held in inventory, for example, the goods are still to be manufactured or will be delivered directly to the customer from a third party.

Revenue is recognised when the goods are delivered to the buyer.

5. Sale and repurchase agreements (other than swap transactions) under which the seller concurrently agrees to repurchase the same goods at a later date, or when the seller has a call option to repurchase, or the buyer has a put option to require the repurchase, by the seller, of the goods.

The terms of the agreement need to be analysed to ascertain whether, in substance, the seller has transferred the risks and rewards of ownership to the buyer and hence revenue is recognised. When the seller has retained the risks and rewards of ownership, even though legal title has been transferred, the transaction is a financing arrangement and does not give rise to revenue.

6. Sales to intermediate parties, such as distributors, dealers or others for resale.

Revenue from such sales is generally recognised when the risks and rewards of ownership have passed. However, when the buyer is acting, in substance, as an agent, the sale is treated as a consignment sale.

7. Subscriptions to publications and similar items.

When the items involved are of similar value in each time period, revenue is recognised on a straight line basis over the period in which the items are despatched. When the items vary in value from period to period, revenue is recognised on the basis of the sales value of the item despatched in relation to the total estimated sales value of all items covered by the subscription.

8. Instalment sales, under which the consideration is receivable in instalments.

Revenue attributable to the sales price, exclusive of interest, is recognised at the date of sale. The sale price is the present value of the consideration, determined by discounting the instalments receivable at the imputed rate of interest. The interest element is recognised as revenue as it is earned, on a time proportion basis that takes into account the imputed rate of interest.

9. Real estate sales.

Revenue is normally recognised when legal title passes to the buyer. However, in some jurisdictions the equitable interest in a property may vest in the buyer before legal title passes and therefore the risks and rewards of ownership have been transferred at that stage. In such cases, provided that the seller has no further substantial acts to complete under the contract, it may be appropriate to recognise revenue. In either case, if the seller is obliged to perform any significant acts after the transfer of the equitable and/or legal title, revenue is recognised as the acts are performed. An example is a building or other facility on which construction has not been completed.

In some cases, real estate may be sold with a degree of continuing involvement by the seller such that the risks and rewards of ownership have not been transferred. Examples are sale and repurchase agreements which include put and call options, and agreements whereby the seller guarantees occupancy of the property for a specified period, or guarantees a return on the buyer's investment for a specified period. In such cases, the nature and extent of the seller's continuing involvement determines how the transaction is accounted for. It may be accounted for as a sale, or as a financing, leasing or some other profit sharing arrangement. If it is accounted for as a sale, the continuing involvement of the seller may delay the recognition of revenue.

A seller must also consider the means of payment and evidence of the buyer's commitment to complete payment. For example, when the aggregate of the payments received, including the buyer's initial down payment, or continuing payments by the buyer, provide insufficient evidence of the buyer's commitment to complete payment, revenue is recognised only to the extent cash is received.

Rendering of Services

10. Installation fees.

Installation fees are recognised as revenue by reference to the stage of completion of the installation, unless they are incidental to the sale of a product in which case they are recognised when the goods are sold.

11. Servicing fees included in the price of the product.

When the selling price of a product includes an identifiable amount for subsequent servicing (for example, after sales support and product enhancement on the sale of software), that amount is deferred and recognised as revenue over the period during which the service is performed. The amount deferred is that which will cover the expected costs of the services under the agreement, together with a reasonable profit on those services.

12. Advertising commissions.

Media commissions are recognised when the related advertisement or commercial appears before the public. Production commissions are recognised by reference to the stage of completion of the project.

13. *Insurance agency commissions.*

Insurance agency commissions received or receivable which do not require the agent to render further service are recognised as revenue by the agent on the effective commencement or renewal dates of the related policies. However, when it is probable that the agent will be required to render further services during the life of the policy, the commission, or part thereof, is deferred and recognised as revenue over the period during which the policy is in force.

14. *Financial service fees.*

The recognition of revenue for financial service fees depends on the purposes for which the fees are assessed and the basis of accounting for any associated financial instrument. The description of fees for financial services may not be indicative of the nature and substance of the services provided. Therefore, it is necessary to distinguish between fees which are an integral part of the effective yield of a financial instrument, fees which are earned as services are provided, and fees which are earned on the execution of a significant act.

(a) *Fees which are an integral part of the effective yield of a financial instrument.*

Such fees are generally treated as an adjustment to the effective yield. However, when the financial instrument is to be measured at fair value subsequent to its initial recognition the fees are recognised as revenue when the instrument is initially recognised.

(i) *Origination fees received by the enterprise relating to the creation or acquisition of a financial instrument which is held by the enterprise as an investment.*

Such fees may include compensation for activities such as evaluating the borrower's financial condition, evaluating and recording guarantees, collateral and other security arrangements, negotiating the terms of the instrument, preparing and processing documents and closing the transaction. These fees are an integral part of generating an ongoing involvement with the resultant financial instrument and, together with the related direct costs, are deferred and recognised as an adjustment to the effective yield.

(ii) *Commitment fees received by the enterprise to originate or purchase a loan.*

If it is probable that the enterprise will enter into a specific lending arrangement, the commitment fee received is regarded as compensation for an ongoing involvement with the acquisition of a financial instrument and, together with the related direct costs, is deferred and recognised as an adjustment to the effective yield. If the commitment expires without the enterprise making the loan, the fee is recognised as revenue on expiry.

(b) *Fees earned as services are provided.*

(i) *Fees charged for servicing a loan.*

Fees charged by an enterprise for servicing a loan are recognised as revenue as the services are provided. If the enterprise sells a loan but retains the servicing of that loan at a fee which is lower than a normal fee for such services, part of the sales price of the loan is deferred and recognised as revenue as the servicing is provided.

(ii) *Commitment fees to originate or purchase a loan.*

If it is unlikely that a specific lending arrangement will be entered into, the commitment fee is recognised as revenue on a time proportion basis over the commitment period.

(c)   *Fees earned on the execution of a significant act, which is much more significant than any other act.*

The fees are recognised as revenue when the significant act has been completed, as in the examples below.

(i)   *Commission on the allotment of shares to a client.*

The commission is recognised as revenue when the shares have been allotted.

(ii)   *Placement fees for arranging a loan between a borrower and an investor.*

The fee is recognised as revenue when the loan has been arranged.

(iii)   *Loan syndication fees.*

It is necessary to distinguish between fees earned on completion of a significant act and fees related to future performance or risk retained. A syndication fee received by an enterprise which arranges a loan and which retains no part of the loan package for itself (or retains a part at the same effective yield for comparable risk as other participants) is compensation for the service of syndication. Such a fee is recognised as revenue when the syndication has been completed. However, when a syndicator retains a portion of the loan package at an effective yield for comparable risk which is lower than that earned by other participants in the syndicate, part of the syndication fee received relates to the risk retained. The relevant portion of the fee is deferred and recognised as revenue as an adjustment to the effective yield of the investment, as in *14(a)* above. Conversely, when a syndicator retains a portion of the loan package at an effective yield for comparable risk which is higher than that earned by other participants in the syndicate, part of the effective yield relates to the syndication fee. The relevant portion of the effective yield is recognised as part of the syndication fee when the syndication has been completed.

15. Admission fees.

Revenue from artistic performances, banquets and other special events is recognised when the event takes place. When a subscription to a number of events is sold, the fee is allocated to each event on a basis which reflects the extent to which services are performed at each event.

16. Tuition fees.

Revenue is recognised over the period of instruction.

17. Initiation, entrance and membership fees.

Revenue recognition depends on the nature of the services provided. If the fee permits only membership, and all other services or products are paid for separately, or if there is a separate annual subscription, the fee is recognised as revenue when no significant uncertainty as to its collectability exists. If the fee entitles the member to services or publications to be provided during the membership period, or to purchase goods or services at prices lower than those charged to non members, it is recognised on a basis that reflects the timing, nature and value of the benefits provided.

18. Franchise fees.

Franchise fees may cover the supply of initial and subsequent services, equipment and other tangible assets, and know-how. Accordingly, franchise fees are recognised as revenue on a basis that reflects the purpose for which the fees were charged. The following methods of franchise fee recognition are appropriate:

(a)   *Supplies of equipment and other tangible assets.*

The amount, based on the fair value of the assets sold, is recognised as revenue when the items are delivered or title passes.

(b)   *Supplies of initial and subsequent services.*

Fees for the provision of continuing services, whether part of the initial fee or a separate fee are recognised as revenue as the services are rendered. When the separate fee does not cover the cost of continuing services together with a reasonable profit, part of the initial fee, sufficient to cover the costs of continuing services and to provide a reasonable profit on those services, is deferred and recognised as revenue as the services are rendered.

The franchise agreement may provide for the franchisor to supply equipment, inventories, or other tangible assets, at a price lower than that charged to others or a price that does not provide a reasonable profit on those sales. In these circumstances, part of the initial fee, sufficient to cover estimated costs in excess of that price and to provide a reasonable profit on those sales, is deferred and recognised over the period the goods are likely to be sold to the franchisee. The balance of an initial fee is recognised as revenue when performance of all the initial services and other obligations required of the franchisor (such as assistance with site selection, staff training, financing and advertising) has been substantially accomplished.

The initial services and other obligations under an area franchise agreement may depend on the number of individual outlets established in the area. In this case, the fees attributable to the initial services are recognised as revenue in proportion to the number of outlets for which the initial services have been substantially completed.

If the initial fee is collectable over an extended period and there is a significant uncertainty that it will be collected in full, the fee is recognised as cash instalments are received.

(c)   *Continuing Franchise Fees.*

Fees charged for the use of continuing rights granted by the agreement, or for other services provided during the period of the agreement, are recognised as revenue as the services are provided or the rights used.

(d)   *Agency Transactions.*

Transactions may take place between the franchisor and the franchisee which, in substance, involve the franchisor acting as agent for the franchisee. For example, the franchisor may order supplies and arrange for their delivery to the franchisee at no profit. Such transactions do not give rise to revenue.

19. Fees from the development of customised software.

Fees from the development of customised software are recognised as revenue by reference to the stage of completion of the development, including completion of services provided for post delivery service support.

Interest, Royalties and Dividends

20. Licence fees and royalties.

Fees and royalties paid for the use of an enterprise's assets (such as trademarks, patents, software, music copyright, record masters and motion picture films) are normally recognised in accordance with the substance of the agreement. As a practical matter, this may be on a straight line basis over the life of the agreement, for example, when a licensee has the right to use certain technology for a specified period of time.

An assignment of rights for a fixed fee or non refundable guarantee under a non cancellable contract which permits the licensee to exploit those rights freely and the licensor has no remaining obligations to perform is, in substance, a sale. An example is a licensing agreement for the use of software when the licensor has no obligations subsequent to delivery. Another example is the granting of rights to exhibit a motion picture film in markets where the licensor has no control over the distributor and expects to receive no further revenues from the box office receipts. In such cases, revenue is recognised at the time of sale.

In some cases, whether or not a licence fee or royalty will be received is contingent on the occurrence of a future event. In such cases, revenue is recognised only when it is probable that the fee or royalty will be received, which is normally when the event has occurred.